D1452985

THE
MALMÉDY MASSACRE

By

JOHN M. BAUSERMAN

 *White Mane Publishing Company, Inc.*

This White Mane Publishing Company, Inc. publication
was printed by
Beidel Printing House, Inc.
63 West Burd Street
Shippensburg, PA 17257 USA

The acid-free paper used in this book meets the guidelines for permanence and durability of the Committee on Production Guidelines for Book Longevity of the Council on Library Resources.

For a complete list of available publications
please write
White Mane Publishing Company, Inc.
P.O. Box 152
Shippensburg, PA 17257 USA

Library of Congress Cataloging-in-Publication Data

Bauserman, John.
    The Malmédy massacre / by John M. Bauserman.
        p.   cm.
    Includes bibliographical references and index.
    ISBN 0-942597-77-X : $19.95
    1. Malmedy Massacre, 1944-1945.   I. Title.
D804.G4B325   1995
940.54′05′094934--dc20   94-32457
                                                        CIP

PRINTED IN THE UNITED STATES OF AMERICA

TABLE OF CONTENTS

AUTHOR'S GLOSSARY, GERMAN RANKS, AND RESOURCES

The research on this book came from two major record groups currently in the Suitland Reference Branch, National Archives and Records Administration at Suitland, Maryland. These record groups are numbered RG 338 and RG 153, and include files headed "6-24 War Crimes" in both record groups. In them are over 14,000 pages of testimonies, depositions, and statements. These materials begin with December 17, 1944 and continue through the Dachau trial in 1946. There are also related record groups located in the National Archives which the serious researcher should consult.

Glossary of frequently used German terms:

Führer — leader

Kampfgruppe — Battlegroup

Mark IV — German medium tank

Panther — German heavy medium tank

Panzer — German tank

SS (Schutzstaffel) — protection squad which later grew into a very powerful, large and perplexing unit. The leader of this unit was Heinrich Himmler, Hitler's accomplice.

SPW (Schützenpanzerwagen) — Standard half-track (armored personnel carrier) used by all combat arms of the German Army and SS.

Tiger — Largest German tank. Almost twice the size of the American tanks

RANKS

AMERICAN		WAFFEN-SS
General	(Gen.)	Oberstgruppenführer
Lieutenant General	(Lt. Gen.)	Obergruppenführer
Major General	(Maj. Gen.)	Gruppenführer
Brigadier General	(Brig. Gen.)	Brigadeführer
No equivalent rank		Oberführer
Colonel	(Col.)	Standartenführer
Lieutenant Colonel	(Lt. Col.)	Obersturmbannführer
Major	(Maj.)	Sturmbannführer
Captain	(Capt.)	Hauptsturmführer
1st Lieutenant	(1st Lt.)	Obersturmführer
2nd Lieutenant	(2nd Lt.)	Untersturmführer

Enlisted

Sergeant-Major	(Sgt. Maj.)	Stabscharführer
1st Sergeant	(1st Sgt.)	Sturmscharführer
Master Sergeant	(M/Sgt.)	Hauptscharführer
Technical Sergeant	(T/Sgt.)	Oberscharführer
Staff Sergeant	(S/Sgt.) (T/5)	Scharführer
Sergeant	(Sgt.) (T/4)	Unterscharführer
Corporal	(Cpl.) (T/3)	Rottenführer
Private First Class	(Pfc.)	Sturmmann
Private	(Pvt.)	SS Mann/Pionier

PREFACE

My interest in the Battle of the Bulge led me to visit the Ardennes area of Belgium in 1985. There I found a discrepancy on one of the many monuments that have been erected to the American fighting men in Belgium during World War II. On a monument in Ligneuville, Belgium, eight men were listed as being shot by the Nazis. One of the men listed was supposedly Abraham Lincoln. The Germans had lined up eight Americans and shot them in the head at point blank range. I found, and later confirmed, that the soldier's name was actually Lincoln Abraham.

My discovery of this inaccuracy led me to conduct a thorough investigation of this shooting and the more well-known atrocity at Malmédy (Baugnez), just north of Ligneuville. The atrocity at Baugnez occurred approximately four kilometers north of Ligneuville, Belgium. Both atrocities were committed by the same German unit, "Kampfgruppe" (Battlegroup) Peiper, part of the 1st SS Panzer Division.

This is the account of what happened at the Baugnez crossroads on Sunday, December 17, 1944. The book covers the events leading up to and following the actual atrocity. After eight years of research, this book will show details that have not previously been chronicled. It is the story of death, luck, and of being in the wrong place at the wrong time.

B Battery was made up of men most of whom came from Pennsylvania, Virginia, Maryland, and West Virginia, with a few men from other states. Those men were thrown together in the inexplicable whirlpool of history. The purpose of my investigation was to develop an accurate description of the Malmédy Massacre and to clarify conflicting information presented previously. This episode of history turned out to be the most infamous atrocity of World War II committed against Americans in the European Theater of Operations.

ACKNOWLEDGEMENTS

My research for this book involved several investigative trips to the massacre site in 1987, 1990, and 1991. In addition, I conducted telephone and personal interviews with survivors, survivors' families, and the families of those soldiers who were killed. In addition, I spent many, many days at the National Archives Suitland Reference Branch in Suitland, Maryland. Other areas of research included the American Battle Monuments Commission in Washington, D.C.; Department of Army Casualty Affairs Office (Graves Registration) in Alexandria, Virginia; the Cartographic and Still Photographic Branch of the National Archives; the Army War College Library at Carlisle, Pennsylvania; and the Captured German Documents Section of the National Archives.

Many people contributed information and research toward this book. A great deal of thanks is given to the survivors of the massacre who contributed their personal stories in both written and verbal form. Special thanks to S/Sgt. Bill Merriken who has given so freely of his time and effort in helping with this research; much of the credit for this book rests on his shoulders.

Relatives of the deceased have helped in many ways. Through our correspondence they have found out what they had not previously known about the death of loved ones.

Without the maps, charts, and photographs, this book would not be complete. These have been supplied by Jay Karamales, author and avid researcher; Hugh Hughes; and Buddy Lovette, who knows more about where to find photographs about the Battle of the Bulge than most. He is also very knowledgeable about military vehicles.

Lt. Col. Barry W. Fowle has contributed valuable editorial assistance for this book.

Col. David Pergrin has been very helpful in giving critical comments with his extensive knowledge about the situation in Malmédy and his insight into the overall situation around the Baugnez crossroads.

Dr. John Wood, History Department, James Madison University, helped with the historical format of the original research paper.

Mr. Charles Stone uncovered several important pieces of history while doing his own research and was happy to share this new information.

Charles MacDonald, former Chief of Military History at the Center for Military History and author of *A Time of Trumpets*, was also a consultant.

Mr. Henri Rogister of Chenee-Liege, Belgium, expedited my search for information in Belgium by sharing his own excellent research on this subject. His knowledge of the area and of languages proved to be invaluable.

Charles Hammer, Archivist of the 285th Field Artillery Observation Battalion, helped with his vast amount of knowledge about the 285th, the men, and their lives. He is the one who is most responsible for not letting the American public forget what these men did for their country.

We owe a tremendous "thank you" to Richard Boylan, Archivist at the National Archives Suitland Reference Branch. Without his help in locating the necessary documents, this book would not be complete.

Finally, but most importantly, I would like to thank retired British Army officer, Major General Michael F. Reynolds. He has contributed as much to the writing of this book as I did. He is regarded as the primary authority on the First SS Panzer Regiment "Leibstandarte Adolf Hitler." His personal study of Kampfgruppe Peiper and its commander, Obersturmbahnführer (Lt. Col.) Joachim Peiper, has gone on for over twenty years and he has been instrumental in giving this book an intuitive look at the men and tactics of Kampfgruppe Peiper. His constant critical thoughts were the driving force behind this endeavor. Although we both realize that the exact truth about the *Malmédy Massacre* will never be known, we do feel that this book gives a true picture of what happened at the Baugnez crossroads on Sunday, December 17, 1944.

INTRODUCTION

The Malmédy Massacre was the most infamous shooting of unarmed American prisoners of war during World War II. I have presented detailed information of the events before, during, and after the Malmédy Massacre. But, in order to place the events in proper perspective, it is first necessary to give a general overview of the time frame and events of Sunday, December 17, 1944. From 6:00 until 9:00 A.M., B Battery closed their installation at Schevenhütte, Germany, in preparation for movement to an unknown location in Luxembourg. They departed in convoy about 9:00 A.M. and stopped for lunch at 11:45 A.M. just north of Malmédy, Belgium. After passing through Malmédy they moved south towards Ligneuville and St. Vith, Belgium. They passed a crossroads village known as Baugnez, approximately 12:45 to 1:00 P.M.

The maps on pages 10 and 11 provide the reader with the geography of this area of Belgium and give a view of the movements of the Americans and the Germans on December 17, 1944. As the Americans moved south on N23, the Germans (Kampfgruppe Peiper) were moving from Thirimont, Belgium, north to Bagatelle, west to the crossroads at Baugnez, and from there were to turn south on N23 to Ligneuville. This occurred because the road from Thirimont to Ligneuville was nothing more than a farm trail and nearly impassable for the heavy vehicles of the Kampfgruppe.

Kampfgruppe Peiper was one of the spearheads of the entire German offensive in the Battle of the Bulge or, as the Belgians say, "The Battle of the Ardennes." The Germans were trying to break out of those narrow, wooded valleys into flatter terrain several miles west. Their objective was the bridges over the Meuse River, several miles to the west.

As the Germans moved north along this road to Bagatelle, the "Spitze" (point) of the Kampfgruppe opened fire on the unsuspecting convoy of B Battery, 285th Field Artillery Observation Battalion. This episode, later to be called "The Malmédy Massacre," rapidly began to unfold after the opening shots.

A little after 1:00 P.M. the convoy came under German attack and the Americans had surrendered by 1:30 P.M. They were searched and then placed in a nearby field south and west of the Baugnez crossroads. At approximately 2:15 to 2:20 P.M., a two- to three-minute barrage of German pistol and machine gun fire killed many of the American prisoners. After this opening burst of fire, some men of Kampfgruppe (Battlegroup) Peiper entered the field to finish off the Americans who were still alive. The Germans were from the Second Platoon, Third Pionier (Armored Engineer) Company, together with SS soldiers belonging to the Penal (disciplinary) section of the 9th Panzer Pionier Company. This part of the atrocity took about ten to fifteen minutes. Shortly afterward, the main body of Kampfgruppe Peiper passed by, heading south toward Ligneuville, and shot into the bodies lying in the field. This continued for about an hour. After the German column passed, the men still alive lay quietly in the field until 4:15 to 4:30 P.M. when most of them attempted to escape. For four days, the survivors struggled back to freedom where they would give their statements about this atrocity.

CHAPTER 1

EIFEL COUNTEROFFENSIVE

THE GERMAN STRATEGY in the Battle of the Bulge, the Eifel Counteroffensive as it is known by the Germans, divided the Allied Forces located in the area of Aachen, Germany, near the Belgian-German border. The Eifel Counteroffensive began on December 16, 1944, and lasted until January 20, 1945. The unit responsible for the Malmédy Massacre was the 1st SS Panzer Regiment, more commonly known as Kampfgruppe (Battlegroup) Peiper, named for its leader Obersturmbannführer (Lt. Col.) Joachim Peiper. This unit belonged to the I SS Panzer Corps, 1st SS Panzer Division.

These units were elements of the 6th SS Panzer Army under the command of SS Oberstgruppenführer (Gen.) Josep (Sepp) Dietrich. This army formed near Paderborn in northwest Germany in the autumn of 1944 and was placed in charge of refitting panzer divisions in preparation for the Eifel Counteroffensive. The I SS Panzer Corps, under the command of Obergruppenführer (Lt. Gen.) Hermann Priess, also took part in the offensive. The 6th SS Panzer Army was responsible for advancing and holding the northern shoulder of the Eifel Counteroffensive. The 1st SS Panzer

Division itself was formed in 1941 by the expansion of elements of the "Leibstandarte," the original Adolf Hitler Lifeguard Regiment, dating back to 1933.

This division served in the Balkans in the spring of 1941, and spent the next several years on the Russian front. The 1st SS Panzer Division, the German title being "Leibstandarte-SS Adolf Hitler," was under the command of Oberführer Wilhelm Möhnke. The 12th SS Panzer Division, the "Hitlerjugend," and the Leibstandarte were elements of the I SS Panzer Corps that joined in the Eifel Counteroffensive.[1] The 1st SS Panzer Regiment (Kampfgruppe Peiper), which was the spearhead of the division, included with it units from the 1st SS Panzer Division.

To better understand the German actions at Malmédy on December 17, 1944, it is important to understand the attitude and mood of the SS at this period in the war. The Waffen SS was the combat arm of the original Schutzstaffel (SS), which translated literally means the "protection squad." It is also necessary to understand the attitude and background of Peiper and the men under his command to comprehend why this atrocity happened. Peiper said that before the offensive the 1st SS Panzer Regiment was based near Cologne and helped remove the dead after an allied bombing raid. He noted, "After the Battle of Normandy, my unit was made up of young fanatical soldiers. A good deal of them had lost parents, sisters, or brothers during the bombing raids. They had seen for themselves the total destruction of the German people, their homes and workplaces; their hatred was such that I could not always keep them under control."[2] The Allied demand for unconditional surrender made the Germans act like cornered animals. The SS were prepared to die for Germany as they were brought up under many years of Nazi propaganda and indoctrination. They were fanatical soldiers, tough and ruthless, fighting for their lives and Germany's existence.

Obergruppenführer (Lt. Gen.) Herman Priess of the I SS Panzer Corps, stated that the Waffen SS was under Reichsführer Heinrich Himmler regarding questions of personnel and "philosophical matters." Peiper's unit was part of the Waffen SS, the combat arm of the SS, and was under the tactical command of the Army. However, Kampfgruppe Peiper was equipped and supplied through the administrative branches of the SS and under SS disciplinary control.[3]

During 1937 some effort was made to teach all SS officers in the military academies the significance of the tactics applied by Genghis Khan. A work by Michael Prawdin, *Genghis Khan and His Legacy*, was issued as source material and each SS graduate from officer candidate school was given a copy. Priess received his copy as a Christmas present from Himmler's office. According to Genghis Khan, the first attack had to carry terror and panic to the remotest part of the campaign. The invaded country was to be paralyzed with fear. The inhabitants should realize that resistance would be futile. Nothing was to remain in the cities except what could be of use to the Mongols.[4]

Reichsminister Rudolph Hess wrote that the Waffen SS was more suitable for the specific tasks to be solved in occupied territory owing to their extensive training in questions of race and nationality. Himmler, in a speech in 1943, indicated his pride in the ability of the SS to carry out criminal acts. He encouraged the SS to be tough and ruthless. He spoke of shooting thousands of Poles and thanked the SS for their cooperation. He extolled ruthlessness in exterminating the Jewish race and later described this process as "delousing." These speeches show that the general attitude prevailing in the SS was consistent with criminal acts.[5]

During preparation for the Eifel Counteroffensive, units of Kampfgruppe Peiper moved into the forest area around Blankenheim, Germany, on December 15, 1944. Kampfgruppe Peiper was to be one of the spearheads of the Eifel Counteroffensive. From Blankenheim, its route was to go through Dahlem, Hallschlag, and Schmid, Germany. From there it was to move into Belgium through the Losheim Gap, with the bridges across the Meuse River being the eventual targets.[6]

The 6th SS Panzer Army issued a field order setting forth the tactical aspects of the Eifel Counteroffensive. This order, drafted by Gruppenführer (Maj. Gen.) Fritz Krämer, Chief of Staff of the 6th SS Panzer Army, was issued to all affected units in mid-December.[7]

This order was the outgrowth of a December 12, 1944, meeting at Bad Nauheim, Germany, among the Führer Adolf Hitler and the army, corps, and division commanders who were to participate in the counteroffensive. During the course of the meeting, Hitler spoke for two to three hours and stated in substance, "that the decisive hour for the German people had arrived; that the impending battle must be won at all costs; that the fighting must be hard and reckless; that the troops must act with brutality and show no humane inhibitions; that a wave of fright and terror should precede the troops; and that the resistance of the enemy was to be broken by terror."[8]

Oberstgruppenführer (Gen.) Dietrich's Army Order of the Day issued on December 14, 1944, stated in substance that "our troops have to be preceded by a wave of terror and fright and that no humane inhibitions should be shown, that every resistance is to be broken by terror." This Army Order of the Day was to be read to the troops immediately prior to the offensive.[9] Dietrich made no mention of the collection points for prisoners of war and one of those present, thinking he had forgotten, asked: "And the prisoners: Where shall we put them?" "Prisoners? You know what to do with them," Sepp Dietrich retorted.[10] How one should interpret this statement is left to conjecture.

Priess, the Corps Commander, held a meeting in early December with about thirty of his unit commanders. Priess noted the speech that Hitler had made at Bad Nauheim and stated that on orders of the Führer, the troops were to fight with reckless brutality.[11]

On December 14, 1944, Oberführer Wilhelm Möhnke, commander of the 1st SS Panzer Division, conferred with Peiper and related to him the substance of Hitler's speech at Bad Nauheim, that "the battle had to be fought without humane inhibitions and one should remember the victims of the bombing terror."[12] At the same time, Peiper received the field order and information concerning disposition of the enemy troops. Upon returning to his command post in the Blankenheim Forest, Peiper ordered his adjutant, Hauptsturmführer (Capt.) Hans Gruhle, to call a commanders' meeting at 4:00 P.M. For two hours prior to the meeting, Peiper studied the material obtained from the 1st SS Panzer Division which, among other items, contained the 6th SS Panzer Army Order directing that a wave of terror and fright precede the German troops. The order said German soldiers should recall the innumerable German victims of the bombing raids. This order emphasized that German troops should use terror to break enemy resistance and should shoot prisoners of war when local conditions of combat so required. Gruhle, on orders issued by Peiper, incorporated this Army Order of the Day into the regimental order.[13]

Sturmbannführer (Maj.) Werner Poetschke held a meeting of the company commanders, 1st Panzer Battalion, Kampfgruppe Peiper, at the regimental command post on December 15, 1944, and told them of the regimental order. The commanders were told to use terror to break enemy resistance and to take no prisoners. Ahead of the troops, Obersturmbannführer (Lt. Col.) Skorzeny's unit, known by the code name "Grief," would destroy communications and spread terror and panic. The troops were to suppress all misgivings and humane feelings. Major Poetschke talked to the assembled groups and Peiper made intermittent comments. Pursuant to Peiper's orders, commanders at all levels held meetings with their subordinates to pass along the plans for the offensive.

Historians have noted that Peiper did ascertain, after reading the 6th SS Panzer Army Order of the Day directing a wave of terror and fright should precede the German troops, that in certain battle conditions prisoners of war (POWs) were to be shot if local conditions of combat warranted it, for example, (1) if POWs could not be guarded, (2) if they were interfering with combat operations, or (3) if they were escaping. However, historians also note that Kampfgruppe Peiper sent over 600 POWs to the rear during the Eifel Counteroffensive.[14]

Peiper was born on January 30, 1915, in Berlin, Germany, the son of an army officer. During his school years he became fluent in the English language and after finishing high school in 1933, he immediately joined a cavalry unit of the SS. This unit escorted dignitaries to many festive Nazi functions such as the Parteitag (Party Day) at Nürnberg. In 1935 he attended the Kriegsschule der SS (officers training school) at Braunschweig. Upon receipt of his commission in 1936, he joined the Leibstandarte (Hitler's Lifeguard Regiment), serving until 1938 when he became Reichsführer Heinrich Himmler's (head of the SS) adjutant and liaison with the Waffen SS (the fighting unit of the SS). Peiper accompanied Himmler everywhere, even to the gassing of inmates in a concentration camp.

In 1940 Peiper returned to the Leibstandarte, which became the 1st SS Panzer Division, and stayed with them until the end of the war. This unit spent most of the war on the eastern front fighting the Russians. Peiper commanded the 3rd Battalion of the 2nd Panzer Grenadier Regiment. This unit was given the nickname "Blow Torch Battalion" after it burned two villages and annihilated the inhabitants. In March 1943, Peiper received the "Ritterkreuz" (Knight's Cross) for distinguished service during the early victories in Russia. He received the German Cross of Gold in May 1943, and in February 1944, the highly desired Oak Leaves to the Ritterkreuz for gallantry during the battle near Shitomir, Russia, in May 1943. For his exploits, Peiper became an Obersturmbannführer (Lt. Col.) in April 1944, and in June of that year he took command of the 1st SS Panzer Regiment, at the age of twenty-nine. "The Führer, besides admiring Peiper both for his daring military ability and their mutual contempt of generals, had an unshakable faith in what he called Peiper's 'fanaticism.' Peiper was, to be sure, a hard-core Nazi, but he was also a cynical realist, a man who had no illusions as to Germany's fate if the war was lost."[15]

While Peiper was a prisoner after the war, he was questioned on his military strategy. He wrote that he organized his battle-group according to the orders he received from Priess. Under these orders he was to reach the Meuse River as soon as possible. "The roads assigned to us were generally known to be bad, but there were few bridges along the way."[16] He decided that his column would be about twenty-five kilometers long. Because the vehicles in the rear would be unable to overtake those in the front due to the bad roads, he placed all combat elements near the front of the column. In order to provide maximum speed and power, he decided that his "SPWs" would proceed as fast as possible until they met resistance. Then the panzers would come up to help destroy the resistance. Following that, the SPWs would again advance. He expected that if all went well, he would need only "Mark IVs" (tanks) and "Panthers" (tanks) along with their panzer grenadiers (armored infantry) to reach the Meuse River. He could move up the heavy "Tigers" (tanks) later.[17]

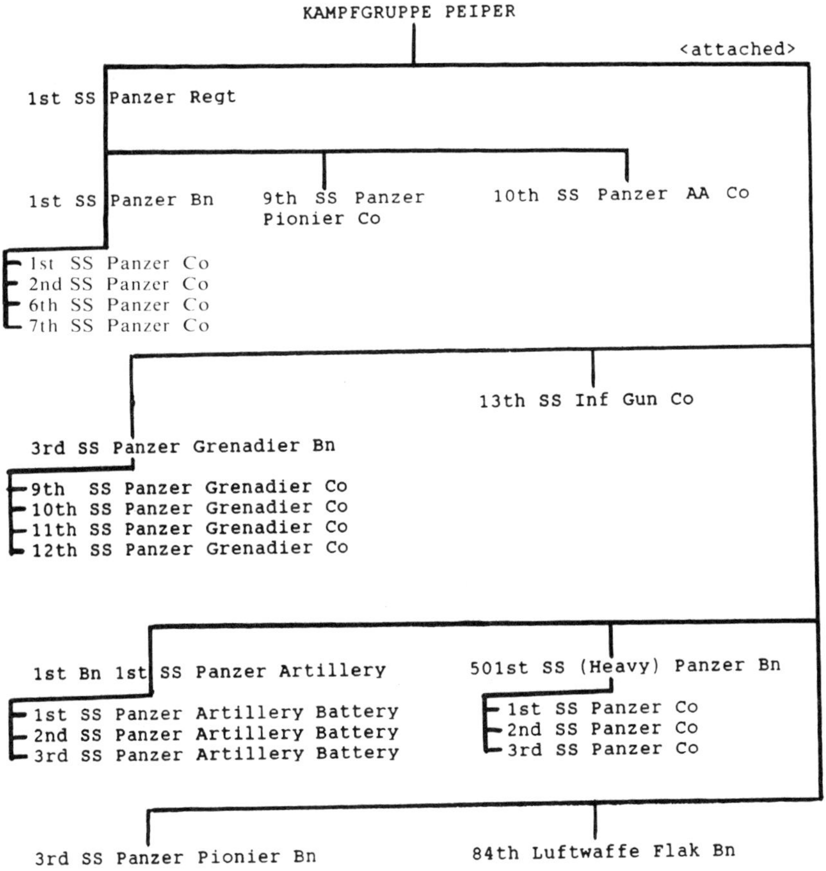
KAMPFGRUPPE PEIPER
<attached>
1st SS Panzer Regt
1st SS Panzer Bn
9th SS Panzer Pionier Co
10th SS Panzer AA Co
1st SS Panzer Co
2nd SS Panzer Co
6th SS Panzer Co
7th SS Panzer Co
13th SS Inf Gun Co
3rd SS Panzer Grenadier Bn
9th SS Panzer Grenadier Co
10th SS Panzer Grenadier Co
11th SS Panzer Grenadier Co
12th SS Panzer Grenadier Co
1st Bn 1st SS Panzer Artillery
1st SS Panzer Artillery Battery
2nd SS Panzer Artillery Battery
3rd SS Panzer Artillery Battery
501st SS (Heavy) Panzer Bn
1st SS Panzer Co
2nd SS Panzer Co
3rd SS Panzer Co
3rd SS Panzer Pionier Bn
84th Luftwaffe Flak Bn

TO/E of Kampfgruppe Peiper at Baugnez

Courtesy of Major General Michael F. Reynolds

By the time the offensive began, a much needed fuel train had not arrived in the I SS Panzer Corps sector. This forced Peiper to make do with the fuel he had until he ran across American gas depots along his route. "Our division intelligence officer had a situation map purporting to show your supply installations. We believed from the information on that map we could capture gasoline at Büllingen and Stavelot."[18] According to his orders, Peiper was not to stop for looting nor was he to bother with isolated pockets of American resistance. The advancing infantry of Dietrich's 6th Panzer Army would mop them up later.

The offensive began at 5:30 A.M. on the morning of December 16, 1944. Peiper finally joined his Kampfgruppe about 2:00 or 2:30 P.M., upset because of the way the battle was going in the Losheim Gap area, where he was supposed to strike once the infantry opened the way. The Kampfgruppe moved out, but the roads were clogged with many German units trying to get to the front. Kampfgruppe Peiper took until 11:00 P.M. on December 16, 1944, to crawl its way into Lanzerath, Belgium, where the 3rd Fallschirmjäger (Parachute) Division was located. In the Kampfgruppe's haste to get to the assigned attack, Peiper ordered the men to move ahead, at all cost. In this movement the Kampfgruppe lost seven vehicles — two Panthers and five SPWs. They ran over mines the Germans themselves had laid in September 1944, in the area of the Gap.

At 4:00 A.M. on December 17, 1944, the Kampfgruppe left Lanzerath, Belgium, with two Mark IVs leading the column followed by a mixture of SPWs, Mark IVs, and Panthers, plus other assorted vehicles. From Lanzerath, the Kampfgruppe raced through Bucholz, Belgium, without opposition and headed toward Honsfeld, Belgium. Near Honsfeld, they followed the rear of a retreating American column. This enabled the Kampfgruppe to enter the village almost undetected. In Honsfeld they captured several men from the 14th Cavalry Group and some from the 612th Tank Destroyer Battalion. The Kampfgruppe shot several of the men from the 612th after they had surrendered. Following the skirmish at Honsfeld, Peiper headed for Büllingen, Belgium.

Peiper gave the following account of his military actions at Honsfeld. "At dawn Kampfgruppe Peiper arrived at Honsfeld and captured a large American group still asleep. In all, the booty consisted of fifty reconnaissance vehicles, including half-tracks, trucks, and fifteen or sixteen anti-tank guns. One mile northwest of Honsfeld we received some small arms fire, but this did not make me unhappy because although there was a slight delay, it allowed the rear vehicles to close up with the rest of the column."[19]

As the Kampfgruppe left Honsfeld and headed for Büllingen, they overran a small airstrip where they supposedly killed one or two of the men they captured. The Kampfgruppe entered Büllingen sometime around 8:00 A.M. on December 17, 1944, where Peiper found an American fuel depot. "We captured 50,000 gallons of gas and used around fifty POWs to fill up our vehicles."[20]

About 9:30 A.M., the Kampfgruppe left Büllingen and moved about three miles farther southwest toward Möderscheid, Belgium, on their assigned route. "The only difficulty was the road through the woods where many of our vehicles got stuck in the mud."[21] At Möderscheid, the Kampfgruppe "overran a small American garrison"[22] before they turned northwest to Schoppen, Belgium, one mile away. Just on the other side of Schoppen they turned onto a muddy farm trail which led two miles across the fields to Ondenval, Belgium. Leaving Ondenval, the Kampfgruppe moved due west one and one-half miles to Thirimont.

At Thirimont, one road led straight ahead to N23, the main road from Malmédy to St. Vith, but it was only a farm trail and was nearly impassable to the heavy vehicles of the Kampfgruppe. Thus Peiper chose to turn north along a secondary road toward the hard-surfaced road (N32) running from Baugnez east through Waimes. N32 was about one and one-half miles north of Thirimont. This secondary road ran parallel to N23 with an undulating field between them. This field was 1500 yards wide, narrowing to 500 yards where the secondary road joined N32 at Bagatelle. Three-quarters of the way along the short distance from Thirimont to Bagatelle, the panzers crested a hill, and N23 came into view 500 yards to the west. At this moment B Battery of the 285th Field Artillery Observation Battalion was moving slowly along the road from Baugnez toward Ligneuville. They were heading south to their bivouac in Luxembourg. (See map on next page.)

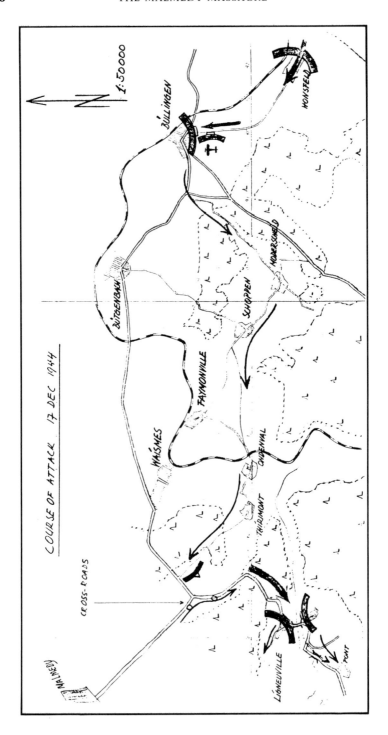

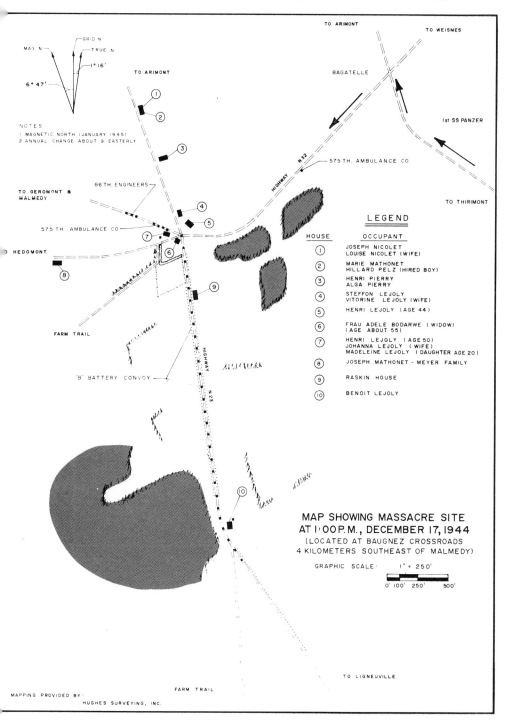

MAP SHOWING MASSACRE SITE
AT 1:00 P.M., DECEMBER 17, 1944
(LOCATED AT BAUGNEZ CROSSROADS
4 KILOMETERS SOUTHEAST OF MALMEDY)

GRAPHIC SCALE: 1" = 250'

0' 100' 250'   500'

L E G E N D

HOUSE   OCCUPANT

(1)   JOSEPH NICOLET
      LOUISE NICOLET (WIFE)

(2)   MARIE MATHONET
      HILLARD PELZ (HIRED BOY)

(3)   HENRI PIERRY
      ALGA PIERRY

(4)   STEFFON LEJOLY
      VITORINE LEJOLY (WIFE)

(5)   HENRI LEJOLY (AGE 44)

(6)   FRAU ADELE BODARWE (WIDOW)
      (AGE ABOUT 55)

(7)   HENRI LEJOLY (AGE 50)
      JOHANNA LEJOLY (WIFE)
      MADELEINE LEJOLY (DAUGHTER AGE 20)

(8)   JOSEPH MATHONET - MEYER FAMILY

(9)   RASKIN HOUSE

(10) BENOIT LEJOLY

NOTES
1 MAGNETIC NORTH (JANUARY 1945)
2 ANNUAL CHANGE ABOUT 9 EASTERLY

GRID N
TRUE N
MAG N
1° 16'
6° 47'

TO ARIMONT

TO ARIMONT

TO WEISMES

BAGATELLE

1st SS PANZER

HIGHWAY N 32

575 TH. AMBULANCE CO.

TO THIRIMONT

86 TH. ENGINEERS

TO GEROMONT &
MALMEDY

575 TH. AMBULANCE CO.

TO HEDOMONT

FARM TRAIL

"B" BATTERY CONVOY

HIGHWAY N 23

TO LIGNEUVILLE

FARM TRAIL

MAPPING PROVIDED BY:
HUGHES SURVEYING, INC.

CHAPTER 2

PEIPER'S MOVEMENTS

I T IS IMPORTANT to note that Kampfgruppe Peiper moved in three groups: the Spitze (point); the command group (Peiper, his infantry and tank commanders); and the main body. The Spitze initially fired on the American convoy. The map on page 22 will give a better understanding of the location of American and German vehicles and personnel.

The Spitze, commanded by Obersturmführer (1st Lt.) Werner Sternebeck, contained two "Mark IVs" and two "SPWs." In each SPW were seven men from the 9th Panzer Pionier (Engineer) Company. These engineers were under the command of Unterscharführers (Sgts.) Held and Lier and were responsible for locating and removing enemy mines found in front of the Spitze.

The Spitze came north on the secondary road and fired across the field into the B Battery convoy which was driving south on N23. The Spitze fired multiple seventy-five millimeter tank rounds and machine gun bursts into the unsuspecting American convoy. The Spitze continued north toward Bagatelle, turned left, and drove west to the crossroads. When the Spitze turned south on N23, they fired into the ditches on both sides of the road as they moved south toward Ligneuville. Some Americans surrendered, others feigned death, and some got up from the ditch to avoid being killed.

As the Spitze moved south, the Germans waved or motioned the prisoners north to the crossroads at Baugnez. When Peiper arrived with the command group, he was extremely irritated that the Spitze had been slowed down and that about half of the American vehicles had been destroyed in the attack. Peiper wanted these vehicles for hauling men and materiel. At that point Peiper told the Spitze to move on to Ligneuville, and he dispatched Untersturmführer (2nd Lt.) Arndt Fischer's "Panther" to go with them.

As the command group of Kampfgruppe Peiper reached the crossroads, they turned south onto N23. Here they stopped for a few minutes, probably leaving behind Sturmbannführer (Maj.) Werner Poetschke to deal with the prisoners, and then moved on to Ligneuville. Behind this group was the 7th Panzer Company and two or three SPWs from the 3rd Panzer Pionier Company.

Who gave the order to shoot the POWs has always been debated. One plausible story is that Peiper told Poetschke, "You know what to do with the POWs," or words to that effect. This type of order could have been interpreted in several ways. As an armored column, the Kampfgruppe was not responsible for POWs. Also the Kampfgruppe was a young and fanatical group which had recently helped clean up a city bombed by an allied air attack. As a result, one can imagine how members of Kampfgruppe Peiper interpreted this type of order.

Meanwhile, various units and vehicles were slowly moving through the area. Road N23 was a main road but barely wide enough for two panzers or SPWs to pass. At the same time, the members of B Battery who had been captured were walking north to the crossroads at Baugnez. Not all of the POWs arrived at the field at the same time. When the prisoners neared the crossroads, they were searched and placed in a field approximately eighty yards south of the crossroads and about twenty yards from Road N23.

Who or what started the firing will never be known. However, seventy percent of the surviving prisoners state that a soldier or officer on the north side of the field fired the first shots.

Joachim Peiper as a
Prisoner of War.

German troops on the offensive.

The soldiers also state that the German officer was either on the road or standing in an open vehicle. According to many previously published accounts, supposedly Sturmmann (Pfc.) George Fleps, in panzer #731, fired the first shots. Fleps was on the south side of the field as far as sixty yards away from the POWs when he fired his shots. Lt. Virgil Lary of B Battery identified Fleps at the Dachau War Crimes Trial in 1946 as the man who fired the first shot. It is hard to understand how anyone could, a year and one-half later, single out and identify a person from a split second observation under combat conditions. None of the other survivors was able to identify any of the Germans.

If one takes into consideration that there were two or more groups of American captives and that they arrived at the crossroads at different times, then Fleps could have fired at a later group of POWs. These men could have been in the process of moving into the southern end of the field just prior to the predetermined shooting of the assembled prisoners.

Because Peiper had ordered his units to keep moving, orders transferred from one part of the regiment to another as they continued on to their destination. Initially there was a conflict as to what part of the Kampfgruppe was to guard the Americans. Probably the first group to have this responsibility were members of the 11th Panzer Grenadier Company (Armored Infantry). Soon they moved south. At this point two SPWs from the 3rd Panzer Pionier (Engineer) Company arrived along with the Penal (Disciplinary) Platoon of the 9th Panzer Pionier Company. These troops then shared the duty of guarding the prisoners.

The first vehicle from the 3rd Panzer Pionier Company to turn south onto N23 was the SPW of Unterscharführer (Sgt.) Max Beutner, leader of the second platoon (see TO/E list of SS personnel). Sturmbannführer (Maj.) Poetschke stopped this vehicle as it reached the field where the first group of POWs were assembled. At this point Poetschke may have told Beutner, "You know what to do with the prisoners." Beutner may have taken this order to mean that the prisoners were to be shot. Beutner's SPW pulled off to the left (east) side of N23 to carry out the orders. After getting out of his SPW, Beutner stopped other vehicles that belonged to his platoon to help him comply with Poetschke's orders.

The first vehicle Beutner halted was the SPW of Unterscharführer Sepp Witkowski. This vehicle pulled up on the right (west) side of N23 just beyond where Beutner's SPW had parked near the southernmost point in the field where the POWs were located. Meanwhile, an SPW belonging to the 11th Panzer Grenadier Company (Armored Infantry) came onto the scene and stopped. An Obersturmführer (1st Lt.) gave an order to the vehicle commander, Unterscharführer (Sgt.) Schuhmacher, to load their seventy-five millimeter cannon. Schuhmacher seemed delighted to shoot the POWs, showing his pleasure by the expression on his face and the way he said, "Marsch, marsch!" This was a common and well-known expression that some officers of the Kampfgruppe always used to indicate satisfaction and pleasure. Schuhmacher, after much shifting and turning, could not get his cannon depressed enough to cover the Americans. He was then sent south toward Ligneuville because his position blocked most of the road making it nearly impossible for the rest of the vehicles to pass.[23]

Meanwhile, other SPWs which had come from the direction of Waimes and Bagatelle halted on road N32. With these SPWs were men from the 9th Panzer Pionier Company, 1st SS Pionier Battalion (see TO/E list on page 129). Obersturmführer (1st Lt.) Erich Rumpf led this unit. As the 9th Panzer Pionier Company arrived, there was no traffic and the road was open.

Several of Rumpf's men dismounted and went to loot the American vehicles. The remainder walked toward the field south of Café Bodarwe where the POWs were assembled. As the Germans returned to their vehicles, they passed Rumpf's vehicle and told him there were many Americans in the field south of the Café. The Germans reached their SPWs and had been there a few minutes when some panzers passed. Most were moving very slowly, almost at walking speed, while several more cut the corner of the crossroads on their way south. Just after some of the 9th Panzer Pioniers passed Rumpf's SPW, Rumpf held a conversation with another officer. After this, Rumpf called most of the men from the Penal (Disciplinary) Platoon and sent them toward the POW field. He sent Unterscharführer (Sgt.) Dorr with the men and told him to report to a person at the field. Dorr sensed that they would probably shoot the captives. After Dorr received his orders, he returned to Rumpf and told him, "This man tells me that I should shoot prisoners of war." Rumpf stated that he assumed that when Dorr returned, he had already passed on the order to the men, assuming that Rumpf would have insisted on the execution of such an order. To ensure the orders were carried out, Rumpf walked to the north end of the field to supervise his troops.[24]

The German version of the sequence of events at the crossroads is not documented because none of the German survivors of Kampfgruppe Peiper will discuss the actions at Malmédy. German pre-trial statements and testimonies given at the war crimes trials seem to indicate that Beutner and Poetschke gave the orders to shoot. However, both of these men were killed later in the war and efforts to confirm these accusations about the massacre have been limited. Therefore, after much research and many visits to the actual massacre site, the author has deduced the sequence of events based upon the available documented German records.

CHAPTER 3

GERMAN VERSION OF THE MASSACRE

PRE-TRIAL STATEMENTS given by the Germans accused of the Malmédy Massacre form the basis of this chapter. The information taken from the German statements supports the American statements as to what occurred during this atrocity. Most of the German statements were taken after days of unauthorized treatment in order to extract information. In 1948, an official commission found firm evidence to consider that many of these men were innocent. Still, many of the statements given by the Germans confirm the American statements.

German soldiers stated that Obersturmführer (1st Lt.) Erich Rumpf, commander, 9th Panzer Pionier Company, and Unterscharführer (Sgt.) Max Beutner, platoon leader of the 2nd Platoon, 3rd Panzer Pionier Company, gave the orders to shoot. Sturmmann (Pfc.) Max Rieder jumped off Rumpf's "SPW" to loot the American vehicles which were parked alongside the road headed south. While walking toward one of the trucks, Rieder noticed Rumpf talking with another officer in front of Café Bodarwe. As Rieder rifled through one of the trucks, Rumpf yelled to him to get his weapon and come. Rieder returned to the SPW, while Rumpf walked to the north end of the field where the captives were standing. When Rieder reached the front of Café Bodarwe, he noticed American prisoners standing in the field to the south of the café. Rumpf and several members of the Penal (Disciplinary) Platoon of the 9th Panzer Pioniers stood in a group to the north of the prisoners. After standing there for about two to three minutes, Rumpf gave an order to the effect of, "Bump off the POWs."[25]

At this time Oberscharführer (T/Sgt.) Wendeleit, Unterscharführers (Sgts.) Helmuth Haas, Willi von Chamier, and Biotta fired their weapons. Rieder fired five shots at an American who hit the ground and did not move. Rieder assumed he was dead. Rieder's story was corroborated by Unterscharführer (Sgt.) von Chamier who said he "received orders from Rumpf to 'bump off the prisoners.'"[26]

As the shots were fired, there were many panzers from the 7th Panzer Company driving around or cutting the corner at the crossroads to continue south on N23. Untersturmführer (2nd Lt.) Heinz Rehagel, platoon leader of 1st Platoon, 7th Panzer Company, was in command of panzer #711 when it arrived at the crossroads, turned left, and slowly drove south about 5 miles per hour. In a field farther to the south he saw Americans standing with hands raised. Rehagel said he received a direct order, and he shot twenty to thirty rounds at the prisoners with the machine gun.[27] He fired low bursts from his machine gun into the group of prisoners and some dropped to the ground. He shot into the few POWs who remained standing until they all dropped.[28]

Oberscharführer (T/Sgt.) Roman Clotten, commander of panzer #723, fired at enemy targets approximately 300 yards before the crossroads at Baugnez. Hauptscharführer (M/Sgt.) Hans Siptrott was in the panzer in front of him as the panzers slowly proceeded to the crossroads. When they turned the corner to head south on N23, Clotten saw captured Americans lined up close together in the field on the right side (west) of the road. Eight SS men in gray uniforms stood in front of them. Clotten believed that they came from the two SPWs parked there. The firing on the POWs began when Clotten reached the hard surfaced road, N23, and started south. Clotten believed that the first shots came from the men in gray. At the first shot, the Americans fell to the ground. Immediately after the first shots, about five of the SS returned to their SPWs. The ones who remained continued to fire at the POWs. As the prisoners were killed, Clotten and Siptrott continued to move south very slowly (walking pace), along with the other advancing panzers.

About twenty yards from the southern edge of the spot where the prisoners were lying, Clotten stopped because all the panzers came to a halt. Siptrott was standing in his panzer turret about twenty to thirty yards ahead of Clotten. Unterscharführer (Sgt.) Erich Dubbert, panzer #713, and Oberscharführer (T/Sgt.) Werner Koch, panzer #712, had stopped behind Clotten while panzer #734, driven by Manfred Thorn, was thirty or forty yards in front of Siptrott's, near house #9.

Immediately after Clotten's panzer halted, gunner Sturmmann (Pfc.) Herman Bock reached for a pistol, which lay in the turret, and stood up on the panzer. He made a half turn to the right and fired several shots at the captives. Even after Bock stopped firing, the other panzers continued to fire at the Americans lying in the field. Just before the panzers moved out, Clotten remembered two men, one of whom was Obersturmführer Rumpf, walking toward the panzers from the direction of the field. Clotten stayed there for about two minutes before heading on south. Members of his crew wanted to stay and loot the American vehicles but the Kampfgruppe continued south on N23.

Hauptscharführer (M/Sgt.) Hans Siptrott, commanding panzer #731, and his loader, Sturmmann George Fleps, gave pre-trial statements. They said they were ordered by Beutner to stop and turn their cannon on the prisoners. Siptrott replied that he did not have enough ammunition. He continued to keep #731 moving very slowly southward. However, he turned around and saw Fleps sitting in the loader slit of the panzer with a pistol in his hand. Siptrott permitted Fleps to shoot because their company commander had made a speech to the company on December 16 in which he said the men were not to take prisoners. When they were thirty yards south of the POWs, Siptrott told Fleps to shoot since it was within the scope of their company commander's order. As Fleps fired two shots at the prisoners, Siptrott saw one of them fall.[29]

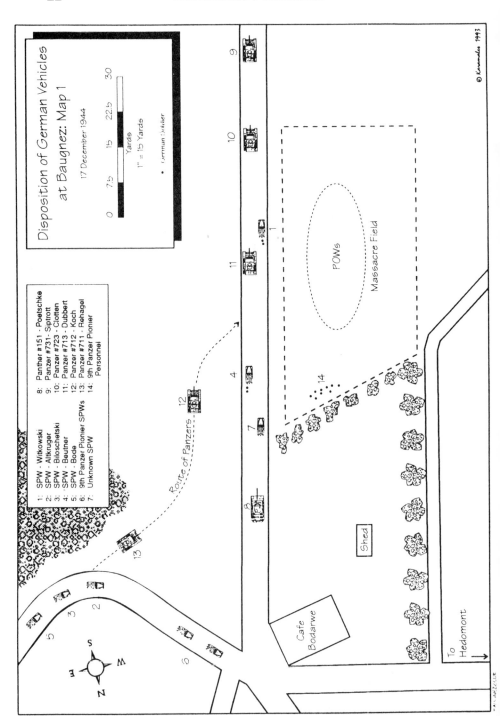

Disposition of German Vehicles
at Baugnez: Map 1

17 December 1944

Yards
1" = 15 Yards
• German Soldier

1: SPW - Witkowski	8: Panther #151 - Poetschke
2: SPW - Altkruger	9: Panzer #731 - Siptrott
3: SPW - Biloschetski	10: Panzer #723 - Clotten
4: SPW - Beutner	11: Panzer #713 - Dubbert
5: SPW - Bode	12: Panzer #712 - Koch
6: 9th Panzer Pionier SPWs	13: Panzer #71 - Rehagel
7: Unknown SPW	14: 9th Panzer Pionier Personnel

Route of Panzers

POWs

Massacre Field

Cafe Bodarwe

Shed

To Hedomont

© Kavander 1993

Fleps supported Siptrott's testimony by stating that #731 was at the head of the platoon followed by Oberscharführer (T/Sgt.) Roman Clotten's panzer. As the panzers turned onto N23, Fleps saw an SPW with its machine gun pointed at the prisoners. Beutner, the SPW commander, approached Siptrott and told him that he, Beutner, had received orders from above to kill the Americans. As they continued south, Siptrott saw a pistol in Fleps' hand, placed his hand on Fleps' shoulder, and ordered him to shoot. Fleps fired a shot at an American standing in the field and saw him fall.[30]

These statements help to corroborate that most of the men in the SPWs and panzers believed that the prisoners were to be shot. Other German statements confirm that orders to shoot the Americans were given prior to the massacre. The shot that Fleps fired probably was at a smaller group of men south of the field. When Fleps fired, the men of the 2nd Platoon, 3rd Panzer Pionier Company, prepared to fire (see TO/E list). At the same time, the 9th Panzer Pioniers at the north side of the field under Rumpf's command also fired when he gave the order. Whether Rumpf's order was the command that started it, no one will ever know. Seventy percent of the survivors say a German in a vehicle at the north end of the field fired the first shots. Approximately two to three minutes after the firing ceased, the remaining panzers slowly moved through the area and headed toward Ligneuville.

Several members of the Pioniers gave evidence that Beutner ordered the prisoners shot. Statements of Unterscharführer (Sgt.) Sepp Witkowski's SPW crew provided evidence that Beutner was one of the men who gave an order to "bump off" the prisoners. This evidence also implicated Rottenführers (Cpls.) Ernst Goldschmidt and Max Hammerer from Beutner's SPW. They initially fired from the vehicles that were directly in front of the prisoners.

Sturmmann (Pfc.) Joachim Hofmann, the driver of Witkowski's SPW, saw eighty to one hundred captured Americans standing in a pasture located south of a café and barn on the west side of the road. He saw a "Panther" and Beutner's SPW there. As Hofmann passed Beutner's SPW, Beutner told Hofmann's crew to get their machine guns ready to "bump off" the prisoners. Hofmann stopped his vehicle, dismounted, and took up a position near the end of the vehicle along with Sturmmann (Pfc.) Gustav Neve. Hofmann had a machine pistol on his waist. Just before the shooting began, the crews of the nearby vehicles were shouting, "Bump them off, bump them off." Hofmann fired four or five bursts, about thirty shots, into the group of prisoners, several of whom were medics. The American prisoners, unarmed and standing with their hands over their heads, were making no attempt to escape. Hofmann said that Rottenführer (Cpl.) Ernst Goldschmidt got out of Beutner's vehicle and stood behind it with Hammerer and Beutner. When the order came to open fire, Hofmann saw both Goldschmidt and Hammerer fire their weapons.[31]

The statements of Sturmmann (Pfc.) Siegfried Jäkel, Pioniers (Pvt.) Heinz Stickel, and Sturmmann (Pfc.) Gustav Neve reinforce Hofmann's statement that Beutner gave an order to shoot. Sturmmann (Pfc.) Jäkel arrived at the crossroads between 1:00 and 2:00 P.M. on December 17, 1944. He observed sixty to eighty American POWs standing in a pasture on the right side of the road. A German SPW belonging to Unterscharführer (Sgt.) Schuhmacher of the 11th Panzer Grenadiers was standing on the road with its cannon pointed into this group. Jäkel's SPW, driven by Hofmann, was stopped by Beutner just beyond the center of the pasture on the right side of the road. Beutner then told the SPW commander, Unterscharführer (Sgt.) Sepp Witkowski, that the American prisoners were going to be shot. Hearing this order the men in Witkowski's SPW loaded their weapons in preparation for firing into them. Jäkel assisted in getting the front machine gun ready and served as a loader. Upon Beutner's command to fire, members of the SPWs in the vicinity began to fire. Jäkel fired approximately seventy-five rounds from the front machine gun, went to the rear machine gun, loaded it, and started firing into the American prisoners.[32]

Sturmmann (Pfc.) Gustav Neve, in Witkowski's SPW, arrived at the crossroads between 1:00 and 2:00 P.M., and turned left in the direction of Ligneuville. Here he saw approximately eighty to one hundred unarmed Americans standing in the pasture with their hands raised. Beutner ordered Neve to stop his vehicle and ordered the men of the crew to load their weapons. Neve dismounted while the other men of his SPW readied their weapons. Neve and Hofmann were standing to the rear of their SPW when the crews of the vehicles cried out, "Bump them off, bump them off." Neve had a fast firing rifle, Hofmann had a machine pistol, and they both opened fire when everyone else did.[33] Sturmmann (Pfc.) Heinz Stickel, also in Witkowski's SPW, fired approximately fifty rounds of ammunition with his machine gun, aiming at the heads of the prisoners. Stickel was sure he killed the prisoners at whom he shot.[34] When the firing stopped, there was a lull for a few minutes as the panzers continued south.

Then came the worst part for the American prisoners. Depositions given by the Americans say that Germans came into the field and shot the wounded POWs. The following German statements from Witkowski's crew confirm this action. Jäkel said he entered the pasture, where he shot four or five wounded American soldiers with a pistol, using only one round and shooting into the heart of each wounded man. After receiving orders, Hofmann moved into the field to render "mercy shots" to those prisoners still alive. He approached two wounded prisoners and fired six to eight rounds into the head of each. Neve entered the pasture and fired a round into the heads of eight or ten Americans who were still twisting and turning on the ground.[35]

As the pioniers moved into the field, Unterscharführers (Sgts.) Wolfgang Altkrüger, Friedel Bode, and Willi Bilochetski pulled up their SPWs near Witkowski's. Sturmmann (Pfc.) Gustav Sprenger was in Altkrüger's vehicle. When this SPW arrived at the crossroads, Sprenger said he saw approximately fifty to eighty American soldiers lying in a pasture. He stopped his vehicle directly across from Beutner's SPW which was parked on the left side of the road. He stood up and saw a group of German officers and soldiers in the field. The prisoners of war who lay in the field were still turning and twisting in their own blood and those nearest the road were moaning in pain. Beutner walked up to Sprenger and said, "Go and shoot those that are still alive," or words to that effect. At that time Sprenger left his vehicle and went into the field with Altkrüger and Bilochetski. All three fired their machine pistols at those Americans who lay on the ground and showed signs of life. Sprenger fired thirty-two rounds into five Americans who had not yet died.[36]

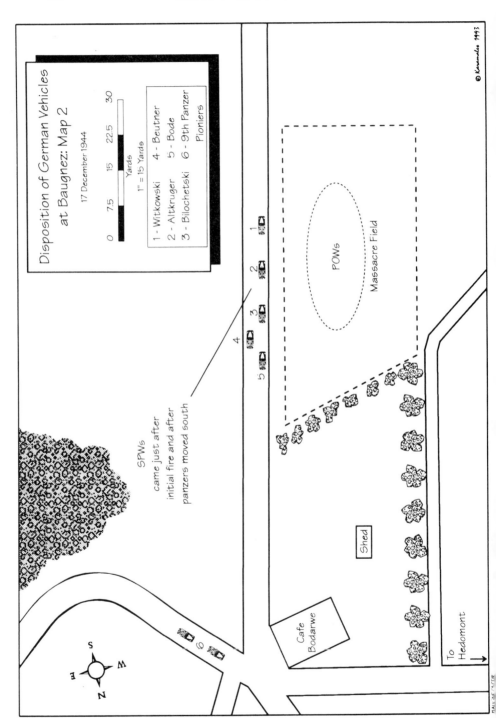

Disposition of German Vehicles
at Baugnez: Map 2

17 December 1944

Yards
1" = 15 Yards

0   7.5   15   22.5   30

1 - Witkowski   4 - Beutner
2 - Altkruger   5 - Bode
3 - Bilochetski 6 - 9th Panzer
                     Pioniers

SPWs
came just after
initial fire and after
panzers moved south

POWs

Massacre Field

Shed

Cafe
Bodarwe

To
Hedomont

© Kuumlee 1993

Members of Bode's SPW gave additional evidence substantiating their role in the massacre. As they parked near the field, Pionier (Pvt.) Johann Wasenberger stated that he "saw Unterscharführer (Sgt.) Friedel Bode talking to Beutner; Bode turned and fired at the prisoners who were lying on the ground, twisting in pain."[37] Wasenberger also stated, "Pionier (Pvt.) Werner Jirassek fired from the SPW into the prisoners with the machine gun. Sturmmann (Pfc.) Herbert Losenski told Wasenberger to fire at one prisoner who was still alive, which Wasenberger did."[38] Sturmmann (Pfc.) Friedel Kies admitted that he fired his machine gun into the prisoners lying in the field. Oberscharführer (T/Sgt.) Willi Schäfer was in an SPW behind Rumpf's vehicle located east of the crossroads on the route to Waimes. In his statement, Schäfer said, "[I] saw Beutner, Hammerer, and Goldschmidt go into the pasture and give 'mercy shots' to the POWs still alive."[39]

While in Russia, the 1st SS gave "mercy shots" to their own badly wounded so they would not be captured by the Russians. These statements not only confirmed the depositions of the Americans but implicated Beutner as the one who gave an order for the "mercy shots." They also implicated the men who gave the "mercy shots." There is some evidence that the members of the Penal Platoon of the 9th Panzer Pionier Company were the main culprits in the shooting even though most of the reprehensible statements belonged to the members of the 3rd Panzer Pioniers.*

It took fifteen to twenty minutes for the Germans to deliver the "mercy shots." The Germans then returned to their vehicles and headed south on N23 to Ligneuville. As the rest of Kampfgruppe Peiper drove south on N23, they fired on the bodies of the prostrate Americans. This action continued intermittently until 4:00 P.M. on December 17, 1944.

During the time these vehicles were passing, several of them stopped, including panzer #624 commanded by Oberscharführer (T/Sgt.) Hubert Huber. Sometime after 3:00 or 3:30 P.M. on

---

* It is interesting to note that many members of the Penal Platoon were not interrogated after the war. Most of the men in this platoon were assigned to the platoon as a punishment for infractions of the SS military code. This platoon was given the most hazardous duties, and life expectancy in its ranks was not long. Many of the members of this platoon died prior to the end of the war.

December 17, 1944, Huber arrived at the crossroads north of Ligneuville. Here he dismounted and saw what appeared to be dead American soldiers lying in the pasture on the right side of the road. He left his "Mark IV" and entered the field where he saw two Americans sprawled on the ground. He moved the body of one of the Americans and the other one underneath stirred. Huber grabbed him by the clothing around his neck and ordered him to get up. It was apparent to him the American was "playing dead." Immediately thereafter he ordered the American, by means of gestures, to remove his field jacket, wrist watch and overshoes. While the prisoner took off his overshoes, Huber shot him in the back of the neck. The prisoner fell to the ground and Huber fired another shot into the prisoner's heart, then one into his chest, and finally one directly in the center of his forehead. When Huber shot the American, the prisoner had no weapon on his body and was not trying to escape.

Prior incidents had put Huber in bad graces with his battalion commander, Poetschke, and his company commander, Obersturmführer (1st Lt.) Benoni Junker. Huber had received orders from them to show no mercy and to shoot everything before his gun barrel. When he found the American soldier alive in the field at the crossroads, Huber wanted to prove to his officers that he was a good soldier and that he obeyed their orders, so he shot the American. On Huber's arrival at Ligneuville he told Unterscharführer (Sgt.) Wrabbitz and Sturmmann (Pfc.) Kurt Dethlefs that he had shot an American soldier. Huber wanted the word to get around to his company and battalion officers that he obeyed orders in shooting everything before his gun. That meant soldiers, civilians, and everything else that was alive.[40]

Unterscharführer (Sgt.) Hans Hillig of the Communications Platoon, Headquarters Company, 1st SS Panzer Regiment, corroborated Huber's statement. He said, "On the afternoon of December 17, 1944 [I] witnessed [Huber's] first shooting of an American POW during the Eifel Offensive. It occurred at the Baugnez crossroads near Ligneuville while the Kampfgruppe stopped for a few minutes. Here [I] saw Huber walk into the pasture on the right-hand side of the road and make an American prisoner get up after kicking him. Huber then ordered the prisoner to take off several pieces of clothing, finally motioning him to turn around, after which he shot him. Huber fired several shots into the prisoner after he fell to the ground."[41]

After the main body of the Kampfgruppe passed, several vehicles that had fallen behind for mechanical reasons came by the crossroads at different times. Panzer #114, a "Panther," commanded by Unterscharführer (Sgt.) Kurt Briesemeister arrived at the crossroads about 3:30 P.M. on December 17, 1944. He stopped about twenty yards east of the crossroads on N32 because of damage to the panzer. South of the crossroads was a field where fifty to sixty American prisoners of war lay. Some were evidently wounded, but most were dead.

During the time Briesemeister was at the crossroads, several of those POWs ran out of the field toward the woods northwest of the field. Many of them ran behind the café and then headed west toward a small patch of woods near the road to Hedomont. One of the panzer crewmen ran after the Americans trying to kill any of the survivors that he could. "Briesemeister shot at them without calling halt. He was not certain whether or not he hit any of them but believed they all succeeded in getting away."[42]

When Briesemeister's crew finished repairing the tank, members of his crew went into the field to loot the bodies. While in the field, they shot some of the Americans who had survived the earlier shootings. Briesemeister went near the field and watched his crew members fire. He then returned to his panzer and, with the aid of a crew member, dismantled the radio operator's machine gun and carried it to the field where the American POWs were lying. He fired about seventy or eighty rounds into the POWs while a crew member held the machine gun on his shoulder. He assumed the greater part of his shots hit the bodies of the Americans lying on the ground.[43]

Just before leaving the scene, Briesemeister pointed his cannon barrel at house #5 (Henri Lejoly's) and fired. Lejoly and another man came running out and told him that they were Germans. Briesemeister gave them a piece of paper with his name and post number so they could be reimbursed for the damage that he caused.[44] Before leaving, the crew of panzer #114 set fire to Café Bodarwe to prevent the Belgian resistance from using the building as a hiding place for guns and ammunition.

After Briesemeister's panzer left, the crossroads became very quiet. In the previous three hours, one of the most infamous atrocities of the war had taken place near this peaceful Belgian crossroads. The depositions of the American survivors on the events of the Malmédy Massacre corroborate the statements of the members of the 1st SS Panzer Regiment, otherwise known as Kampfgruppe Peiper.

The Germans tried to condone what happened at Baugnez. One explanation alleges that ground fog partly concealed the Americans as the main body of Kampfgruppe Peiper approached the crossroads. The Germans thought the Americans were armed and thus fired on them. The Germans said they did not know the Americans were prisoners since the distance and the ground fog made it too difficult to recognize anything. Another story concocted by the Germans stated that while the German guards watched, the American POWs were jostling around, stomping their feet trying to stay warm. One of the guards possibly thought the prisoners were moving too much, so he fired a warning shot which went low and hit an American. This caused a major movement by the POWs. When 1st Lt. John Munzinger (B Battery) shouted, "Stand fast," the Germans interpreted this as a signal for them to make a break and thus the Germans opened fire. Based on existing testimony, this theory seems farfetched at best. The other reasons given by the Germans are even more preposterous, such as the POWs supposedly made a mass break for freedom or they grabbed their weapons and attempted to do battle with the few Germans guarding them.

After the war, members of Kampfgruppe Peiper were found in various allied detention camps and brought to Dachau for trial as war criminals. However, several who took an active part in the shooting at Baugnez were never brought to trial because the prosecution felt they had enough men of Kampfgruppe Peiper to try. In addition, many of the perpetrators had been killed before the end of the war. Beutner and Witkowski were killed at Stoumont a few days after the massacre and Poetschke, as previously mentioned, was killed in Hungary shortly before the end of the war.

On May 16, 1945, seventy-four suspects were brought to trial before an American military court at Dachau. Of the seventy-four suspects, forty-three were sentenced to death and twenty-two were sentenced to life imprisonment. Of the remaining members of the Kampfgruppe, two received twenty years, and five received ten years imprisonment. One of the Kampfgruppe was returned to France for crimes supposedly committed there and was acquitted. If one researches the trial, one will see it was a pretense of justice. Of the total number of men tried, only thirty were involved in the shooting of American prisoners at the Baugnez crossroads.

Peiper was sentenced to death and incarcerated at Landsberg Prison, Landsberg am Lech, Bavaria. On April 12, 1948, the Counter Intelligence Corps received information from reliable sources that former members of the Kampfgruppe would attempt to liberate their commander. Five Germans would travel to Landsberg Prison dressed in United States army uniforms. Before they arrived, the impostors would place a phone call to prison officials stating that five members of the War Crimes Commission were being sent to question Peiper. Once in the prison, the five would ask to see Peiper and one other significant defendant. As soon as Peiper was with them, the Germans would attempt to overcome the guards and liberate their former leader and other condemned comrades. This plan took shape in Munich during March and included Peiper's wife who was in constant contact with members of this group.

The American guards at the prison were alerted and a guard, armed with a machine-gun, was placed in a concealed location covering the entrance. Everyone entering the prison was personally identified and searched before being allowed to enter. This attempt to break Peiper out of prison never came about for whatever reasons. However, it does show how much Peiper was thought of by his former comrades.

Due to the political situation in the early 1950s, none of the death sentences was carried out and all of the men who were convicted were paroled. Papers found in the National Archives show there were several reasons for the commutation of the sentences. First, many felt the defendants had spent enough time in prison; second, there were considerable differences of opinion between the different review boards examining this issue; third, both the United States Senate 1949 Baldwin Sub-Committee hearings and subsequent investigations in Germany raised questions about improprieties prior to and during the trial at Dachau. Only 30% of those charged were involved in the shootings at the Baugnez crossroads, while the rest were charged for atrocities at other places during the attack. Several of these shootings were not proved.

Peiper was released from prison, just prior to Christmas, in December 1956, the last of the Kampfgruppe Peiper personnel to be released. On July 14, 1976, Peiper was killed in Traves, France, by an unknown group, "The Avengers." They set his house on fire and slashed the local fire company's hoses. Peiper died in the fire and the subsequent investigation proved that the body pulled from the burned out rubble was definitely Peiper.

CHAPTER 4

B BATTERY

History of B Battery 285th FAOB

B Battery was part of the 285th Field Artillery Observation Battalion which was activated at Camp Gruber, Oklahoma, on January 11, 1943. It was cadred from the 8th Field Artillery Observation Battalion and supplied with men from Fort Meade, Maryland; Fort Lee, Virginia; and New Cumberland, Pennsylvania. The battalion went through training cycles and on June 6, 1943, went to the Louisiana Maneuvers. On August 18, after the maneuvers, the battalion moved to Fort Sill, Oklahoma, to take over the difficult task of being the school battalion. On May 11, 1944, the 285th commenced their own training for overseas assignment. The battalion passed the many tests successfully and departed for the Port of Embarkation on August 11, 1944. They stayed at Camp Shanks, New York, for four days prior to departing through the Port of New York. They sailed aboard the vessel *SS Mormac Moon* on August 19.

The 285th arrived in Cardiff, Wales (United Kingdom) on September 1, 1944. They transferred to a train and moved to Stockton House Manor, Codford, Wiltshire, where they stayed until September 16. They were transferred to Puddlestown, then to Dorchester, and finally to Weymouth where they boarded a Landing Ship Tank (LST) for the trip across the English Channel. The 285th, less B Battery and a part of A Battery, arrived on Omaha Beach, Normandy, France, on September 18, 1944. B Battery and the rest of A Battery rejoined the battalion the next day and by the evening of September 19, the entire battalion was in bivouac near Colleville sur mer, France.

During the next month, B Battery bivouacked in many towns and villages across France, Luxembourg, and Belgium. On October 15, 1944, they set up camp in Zeifall, Germany. On December 2, 1944, they then moved to Schevenhütte, Germany. From this location they left on their fateful journey into history. The date was Sunday, December 17, 1944.

B Battery Movements on December 17, 1944

On December 16, 1944, at 6:00 A.M., Capt. Leon T. Scarbrough, Commander of Battery B, departed Schevenhütte, Germany. In the vehicle with him were S/Sgt. Orsini, T/4 Hinkel, Cpl. Norfleet, Pvt. Romanoski, and Pvt. Oxford. Before they left the battalion, Executive Officer Lt. Ksidzek, and Capt. Scarbrough determined the destination of B Battery and the route that Lt. Ksidzek was to use to bring the Battery the following morning. Capt. Scarbrough reported to the VIII Corps Artillery Headquarters on the morning of December 17, about 9:00 A.M., and he was instructed to report to the 4th Division Artillery in Luxembourg. Before Capt. Scarbrough left VIII Corps, he reported to the Commanding Officer of the 16th Field Artillery Observation Battalion who gave him survey data and general instructions regarding the area in Luxembourg. Capt. Scarbrough left instructions at the 16th Field Artillery Observation Battalion for B Battery to proceed on to Luxembourg.[45]

A route-marking party consisting of Lt. Geier, S/Sgt. Kesterton, T/4 Paul, Pfc. Farmer, and Pfc. Kennedy preceded B Battery by about two hours and got safely to Luxembourg. As the route-marking party moved through, it picked up Pvt. Romanoski whom Capt. Scarbrough had left as a guide for Lt. Geier.[46]

The remainder of the Battery left Schevenhütte, Germany, about 8:00 A.M. on December 17, 1944, en route to an unknown bivouac in Luxembourg. The Battery convoy consisted of about twenty-six vehicles, including weapons carriers, 6 x 6 trucks, jeeps, and three-quarter ton vehicles. The convoy was divided into two serials of about thirteen vehicles each. Capt. Roger Mills led the first serial accompanied by Lt. Virgil Lary in a jeep driven by Cpl. Ray Lester. 1st Lt. Perry Reardon led the second serial.

Their route to Luxembourg went through the towns of Rott and Raere, Germany, and the towns of Eynatten, Eupen, and Malmédy, Belgium, in an area known as the "Haute Fagnes." About noon, the Battery halted north of Malmédy for lunch. According to T/5 Thomas Bacon, "Lunch for some of the men consisted of hash, peas, pineapple, coffee, bread, and butter."[47]

T/4 Luke Swartz and his buddy T/5 Ernest Bechtel had a rather prophetic conversation as the two finished lunch and prepared to board their vehicles. The story below was told to the author in a letter from Ernest Bechtel in 1989.

> My buddy, T/4 Luke B. Swartz ASN 33497309, who back in the states before the war was also my neighbor, living less than a quarter mile across the fields, told me minutes before Battery B pulled out on its way to annihilation that this would be our last convoy.
>
> I was about to climb aboard truck B-26 when I noticed Luke standing with head bowed at the rear of B-25.
>
> "Why don't you ride with me on B-26," I asked him.
>
> "No, I'll ride on one of the trucks with a tarp. It's beginning to sleet and B-26 has no tarp. Besides, this is my last day anyway. Ernie, I'll not be going home. Something terrible is going to happen to most of us today, but you'll be going back so tell the folks back home I love them."
>
> "What the hell are you talking about," I shouted.
>
> "Most of us will be killed but you'll get through," he repeated.
>
> "Don't talk so damn foolish. Nothing that bad is going to happen," I replied.
>
> Without another word Luke climbed aboard a truck several trucks ahead of B-26.
>
> With those words the convoy moved out and I never saw him again. It was not until December 18 that I learned Luke had died in the field at Malmédy. I sat down and wept in both sorrow and anger.[48]

The convoy moved out after lunch and, after traveling a few miles, entered Malmédy, Belgium. Four vehicles carrying twenty-seven men of the B Battery column halted in Malmédy because Sgt. Barrington suddenly became violently ill with food poisoning and needed medical attention. In the wire truck, B-26, were T/5 Arndt, Pfc. Bechtel, Pfc. Schaaf, Pfc. Bersinski, Pvt. DePaulo, Pvt. Grath, Pvt. Kellum, Pvt. Stewart and Sgt. Barrington. The route-marking truck carried Sgt. Matthews, Cpl. Lorson, T/5 Camp, T/5 Poorman, and Pvt. Smith. In the Battery maintenance vehicle were S/Sgt. Albertson, T/4 Whitmer, T/5 Sondergard, Pvt. Swan, and Pvt. Young. Lt. Ksidzek, 1st Sgt. Iverson, Sgt. Funk, T/5 Harnack, T/5 Boggs, T/5 Forte (Battalion Medical Detachment), and Pfc. Stevens rode in the Battery Commander's vehicle. Pfc. Panzer from the medical detachment joined this group of vehicles to give medical attention to Barrington and remained with these vehicles.[49]

Little did these men realize how lucky they were. It is unknown why all four vehicles left the convoy and not just Barrington's vehicle.

After leaving Barrington at an aid station in Malmédy, these vehicles continued south trying to catch up with their convoy. They had driven less than a half mile when an out of control jeep came roaring toward them. Somehow the driver managed to avoid a collision and stop his jeep. The driver of the jeep was incoherent but several times he clearly mentioned the word "Krauts." An officer riding with him had been shot through the neck. After a brief conversation between Lt. Ksidzek and the wounded officer in the jeep, the trucks moved out once more only to be halted by men of the 291st Combat Engineer Battalion who said, "We're going to blow this row of trees and dump them across the road. Once you're through you cannot return."[50]

In a frantic effort to rejoin the rest of the convoy, Lt. Ksidzek, the highest ranking officer in the four vehicles, ordered the vehicles to move out. As the vehicles approached the crossroads village of Baugnez, which lies at the top of a long gentle hill, they suddenly encountered seventy-five millimeter and small arms fire coming from their left front. They also heard heavy machine gun fire and decided to turn back. While some returned the fire, the trucks managed to turn around and head back toward Malmédy.

With the road into Malmédy blocked, T/5 Arndt, driver of B-26, sought an alternate route. Disregarding the possibility of land mines, he took off cross-country until he got back into Malmédy. These men later made it back to Waldheim and Battalion Headquarters.

Earlier, at the southern end of Malmédy, Lt. Lary of B Battery and Capt. Mills from battalion headquarters were at the head of B Battery's convoy in a jeep driven by Cpl. Lester. They stopped and talked to the commanding officer of the 291st Combat Engineer Battalion, Lt. Col. David Pergrin. The 291st was the only unit of any size in Malmédy, making Pergrin the ranking officer in the immediate area. Pergrin advised Lary and Mills to "head west toward Trois Pont and from there south to St. Vith and on to Luxembourg."[51] He suggested this route because there had been recent reports from his outposts sighting a large German armored column in the immediate vicinity. Disregarding Pergrin's advice, Lt. Lary's jeep continued south on route N32/N23, passed by a 291st roadblock, and went up the long, gradual hill to the crossroads at Baugnez. "There Pfc. Homer D. Ford of C Company, 518th Military Police Battalion, was waiting to direct part of the Seventh Armored Division, south to St. Vith, Belgium. Ford waved B Battery through Baugnez, onto N23 toward Ligneuville and St. Vith. It was about 1:00 P.M. Sunday, December 17, 1944."[52]

At the same time that B Battery's lead vehicles headed south toward Ligneuville and St. Vith, the Germans of Kampfgruppe Peiper were moving north on a parallel road from Thirimont to Bagatelle (see map page 11). As the "Spitze" (point), consisting of two "Mark IV" tanks and two "SPW" armored personnel carriers, moved along this secondary road, they spotted B Battery's column headed south. The Germans opened fire with seventy-five millimeter shells from their panzers, and with machine gun fire from the SPWs.

The first three or four vehicles of the convoy were hidden by the terrain from the view of the Spitze. When the Germans opened fire, the men of B Battery did not realize what was happening. As soon as they realized they were being fired upon by tanks, they stopped their vehicles and jumped into the ditches that ran along both sides of N23.**

T/5 Tom Bacon, whose vehicle was halfway back in the column, heard machine gun fire on his left. The column of trucks stopped and were raked with direct fire. The bullets whistled past his ears. The men left the truck without being hit except for Pfc. Carl Stevens, who was hit in the left shoulder. Bacon fired two shots with his carbine and found that it would not work on automatic. He then took T/4 John Rupp's M-1 and shot about four rounds whenever he saw a muzzle flash. Bullets bounced off of the road in front of him and went over his head. A small caliber shell burst just across the road from him, and he kept looking for something to shoot. Pfc. David Murray was attempting to patch up Stevens, so Bacon gave him a penknife to cut Steven's clothing. Suddenly Rupp shouted, "Bacon, get your head down."[53] Panzers were coming down the road toward the Americans' position.

Pvt. R. L. Smith, the switchboard operator, was in the back of B-24 with T/5 Ted Paluch and T/4 Irvin Sheetz. Sitting up front was T/4 Thomas Watt with T/4 Alan Lucas driving. This truck was approximately fifty yards south of the crossroads (see map page 39). They heard a lot of firing and thought it was an air raid, so they got out of the truck. All of a sudden tracer bullets started to hit around them. They got down behind the truck but found it provided very limited cover, so they moved to a little ditch on the right (west) side of the road. After a few minutes they saw a panzer coming down the road with its muzzle pointed directly at them. They saw it was useless to run and they decided to give up. Smith's group climbed up out of the ditches and surrendered. In a few minutes they all were lined up with their hands in the air.

** It has long been misinterpreted as to how these vehicles were fired upon and why they did not continue south to Ligneuville and escape. In an attempt to answer that question, during July 1990 the author and Major General M. F. Reynolds toured the site and drove the little farm trail from N23 to Thirimont (0.8 miles). As we sat on top of the hill opposite N23 and southeast of where the first vehicles of Battery B had been located, we could clearly see N23. We concluded that the 10th SS Panzer Grenadiers had been ordered to go directly from Thirimont to N23 by this farm trail and then to Ligneuville. As they tried to get across the marshy area at the bottom of the little valley between Thirimont and N23, they saw and heard their comrades in the Spitze fire on B Battery. Still in Thirimont, the 4th Platoon (the heavy weapons platoon) opened fire with their mortars. Mortar fire had been reported by several men of B Battery and since the Spitze's two SPWs and two Mark IVs had no mortars, this theory seems plausible.

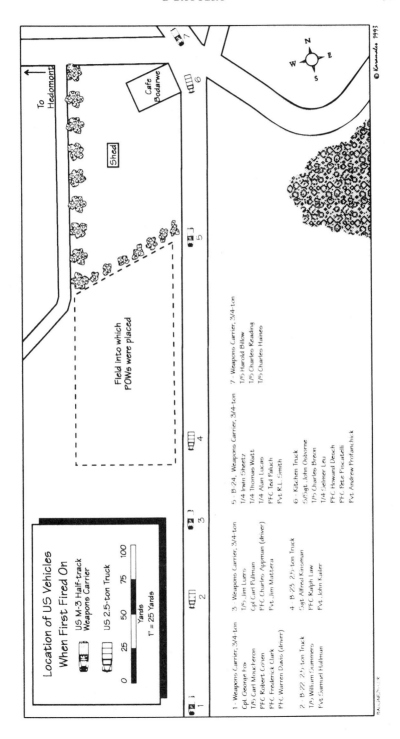

Location of US Vehicles
When First Fired On

US M-3 Half-track
Weapons Carrier

US 2.5-ton Truck

Yards
0   25   50   75   100
1" = 25 Yards

To
Hedomont

Shed

Cafe
Bodanne

Field into which
POWs were placed

1 - Weapons Carrier, 3/4-ton
Cpl. George Fox
T/5 Carl Maucheron
PFC Robert Cohen
PFC Frederick Clark
PFC Warren Davis (driver)

2 - B-22 2.5-ton Truck
T/5 William Summers
Pvt. Samuel Hallman

3 - Weapons Carrier, 3/4-ton
T/5 Jim Luerts
Cpl Carl Pullman
PFC Charles Appman (driver)
Pvt. Jim Matterra

4 - B-23 2.5-ton Truck
Sgt. Alfred Kinsman
PFC Ralph Law
Pvt. John Kailer

5 - B-24, Weapons Carrier, 3/4-ton
T/4 Irwin Sheetz
T/4 Thomas Watt
T/4 Alan Lucas
PFC Ted Paluch
Pvt. R.L. Smith

6 - Kitchen Truck
S/Sgt. John Osborne
T/5 Charles Breon
T/4 Selmer Leu
PFC Howard Desch
PFC Pete Piscatelli
Pvt. Andrew Profanchuck

7 - Weapons Carrier, 3/4-ton
T/5 Harold Billow
T/5 Charles Reading
T/5 Charles Haines

© Kennedies 1993

Another panzer came from the front end of the column past them. There were about five or six German soldiers with rifles who came to search Smith's group. After the search, they marched these new prisoners of war back to the crossroads and kept them there for about five or six minutes. Then they marched Smith and his buddies back to where they were first captured and searched them again.[54]

During this second search, about eight panzers came south from the crossroads. As they stood there, one of the panzer commanders ordered Smith's group to get back off the road and into the field. They went through the barbed wire fence into the field. There were forty or fifty POWs in the field at that time. They milled around for about five or ten minutes, wondering what was going to happen. Finally, the Germans brought an SPW through the field and across the road in front of the prisoners. The crew tried to jockey the SPW so their cannon could be depressed far enough to cover the Americans. After a while they gave up and this SPW moved southward. While the Americans were waiting in the field, two medics, Cpl. Ralph Indelicato and a medic from another outfit, carried Stevens, who was still bleeding from his shoulder wound, into the field from the road.

Near the rear of the convoy, T/5 Charles Appman was driving a weapons carrier. This vehicle was the fourth or fifth vehicle from the rear. The truck in front of Appman stopped, and so did Appman. The machine gun bullets were coming fast and all the occupants in Appman's weapons carrier dove in the ditch on the west side of N23. They stayed in the ditch approximately ten minutes while shells dropped in the field a few yards away. They then decided to crawl along the ditch toward the end of the convoy. After crawling about twenty-five yards, they came to a dead end because of a culvert. Appman told the men to get rid of their letters and personal effects. Some of the Americans tore up their letters and stuffed them in the culvert. They heard a panzer coming down the road, firing as it came. The panzer aimed its machine gun at Appman's men and motioned for them to come out on the road. The panzer continued down the road and left them standing there. Another SPW came out of the field, which was on the opposite side of the ditch that Appman had been in. This vehicle turned left and continued down the road. Thereafter some tanks and half tracks came west on the highway from the direction of Waimes, turned left on highway N23, and proceeded south in the direction of St. Vith.[55]

According to Cpl. Ted Flechsig, who was in the ditch on the east side of the road, when the Germans arrived they made everyone get up, put their hands over their heads, and walk down the road toward the crossroads. Several men of B Battery tried to play dead but the Germans yelled at them and put a couple of shots in their backs if they did not get up. With that, everyone else who was feigning death surrendered.

Cpl. George Fox was in the back of a weapons carrier, the sixth vehicle from the end of the convoy, sitting on duffel bags. With Fox were Pfc. Robert Cohen and T/5 Carl Moucheron. The driver of the weapons carrier was Pfc. Warren Davis and riding beside him was Pfc. Frederick Clark.[56] This vehicle was about 150 yards south of the intersection when they were fired on. The entire column stopped, including the vehicle in front of Fox. Fox's vehicle stopped and all the men jumped out and took cover in a ditch on the right (west) side of the road. The firing continued, and the next thing Fox remembered was that more panzers approached the intersection on a road from the east. When Fox first saw them he thought they were American tanks. The lead vehicle in this column entered the intersection, turned left, and headed south along N23. When this vehicle came around the corner toward this small group, Fox noticed that it had the wide tracks of a German panzer and realized his mistake. However, the panzer did not fire as it came down the road from the intersection.

When the panzer was about halfway to Fox's group, the men stood up and raised their arms in surrender. Just as the front end of the tank approached the rear end of the weapons carrier, these men started walking out of the ditch onto the road with their hands raised. Cohen, Moucheron, and Davis were walking three abreast; Fox and Clark were to the left rear. At this instant, the lead panzer directed a burst of machine gun fire at these men. It missed the men in front but Clark was hit in the chest and fell to the ground. Fox glanced back and saw that Clark had been killed instantly. A couple of German soldiers were watching from the turret of the tank and they motioned the men up the road in the direction of the crossroads. The tank continued moving southward. With his hands still raised, Fox walked to a point about halfway to the crossroads where other American soldiers were being searched, then ordered into the field on the west side of the road.[57]

Other accounts of how the POWs came to the field are similar. Pfc. Mario "Boots" Butera was driving with 1st Lt. Perry Reardon and M/Sgt. Eugene Lacy in a weapons carrier. This vehicle led the second part of the ill-fated convoy. Butera, Lacy, and Reardon took cover in the ditch running alongside the road until they realized the hopelessness of the situation. Lt. Reardon said, "We might as well give up." Butera gave Sgt. Lacy a white handkerchief, which he tied to his carbine and started waving. The enemy ceased firing and the three Americans waited the approach of two Mark IV panzers. As the panzers approached, the crews motioned Butera, Lacy, and Reardon to come forward with arms raised.

The panzers then continued along the road as other German soldiers placed the Americans into a group of approximately seventy-five prisoners. A German infantryman dressed in a regulation green uniform, armed with a rifle and a knife attached to his belt, wearing a peaked cap and black leather boots, guarded them.

The POWs then marched forward about twenty yards. As they stood watching, more panzers came out of the woods. The prisoners were ordered to enter the field on the right side (west) of the road by climbing a barbed wire fence about four feet high. They stood in the pasture for about ten or fifteen minutes, wondering what the Germans' next move would be. A German panzer emerged from the woods on the left and approached to within twenty yards. A crewman was standing in the turret and was armed with a submachine gun. His dress was not fully discernible as he stood in the turret. The POWs were motioned to move back about twenty yards from the road. After the Americans were in the field, a civilian came from Café Bodarwe (house #6), walked up to one of the German soldiers, and spoke to him. This was probably Henri Lejoly, who was not necessarily pro-German but sided with whoever was in charge.[58]

Meanwhile, men at the front of the column, located just south of house #10, were enacting their own scenario. When mortar and machine gun fire began, Lary, Mills, and Lester got out of their vehicle and took cover in the ditch that ran along the west side of highway N23. An old woman was standing in front of house #10 and, strangely enough, according to the men, the shelling did not seem to bother her a bit.

As machine gun fire tore into the tarpaulin of his two and one-half ton truck, T/5 Carl Daub thought at first it was an airplane strafing. When the truck came to a stop behind a house, Daub and the other soldiers in the truck jumped into the ditch on the right side (west) of the road. The men moved from the ditch to a wood-pile north of house #10 on the east side of the road. These men included S/Sgt. Donald Geisler, Pvt. Louis A. Vairo, Cpl. Michael J. Sciranko, and T/5 Howard W. Laufer. While the men were lying behind the woodpile and in the ditch, they debated as to where the firing was coming from and who could get a clear shot.[59]

The Americans were there a few minutes when a jeep came roaring up the road from the south. The two men in it stopped and were told to go to Malmédy and get some help. A few minutes later one of the B Battery men said, "Here comes an American tank." Most of the men in that area stood up, but then realized that the tank was a German panzer. The panzer fired some machine gun bursts at the men in the ditches. As the panzer got closer, its commander waved his hands for the Americans to go north, back toward the crossroads. At first they did not want to put their hands up so the panzer fired a few machine gun bursts at the group. The Americans immediately raised their hands.

A panzer crew member pointed his pistol at Lt. Lary, who was on the west side of the road standing in front of one of the trucks. Seeing he was about to be shot, Lary leaped behind the truck. Having lost his target, the German noticed another man close by, probably Capt. Mills, and fired at him instead.[60]

As Daub, Lary, Geisler, and others walked north back toward the crossroads several panzers came by. The commander of the first panzer had an "Iron Cross" around his neck. This panzer went on by, and a second came abreast of Daub. A German leaned down and took watches and gloves from some of the Americans. As this group walked back north to the crossroads, some B Battery men were lying on the bank of the ditch, presumably dead. Some of

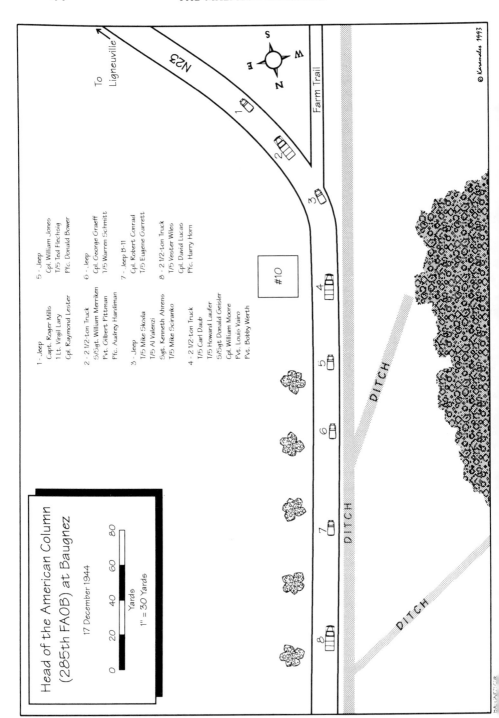

Head of the American Column
(285th FAOB) at Baugnez

17 December 1944

Yards
1" = 30 Yards
0   20   40   60   80

1 - Jeep
Capt. Roger Mills
1 Lt. Virgil Lary
Cpl. Raymond Lester

2 - 2 1/2-ton Truck
S/Sgt. William Merriken
Pvt. Gilbert Pittman
Pfc. Audrey Hardiman

3 - Jeep
T/5 Mike Skoda
T/5 Al Valenzi
Sgt. Kenneth Ahrens
T/5 Mike Sciranko

4 - 2 1/2-ton Truck
T/5 Carl Daub
T/5 Howard Laufer
S/Sgt Donald Geisler
Cpl. William Moore
Pvt. Louis Vairo
Pvt. Bobby Werth

5 - Jeep
Cpl. William Jones
T/5 Ted Flechsig
Pfc. Donald Bower

6 - Jeep
Cpl. George Graeff
T/5 Warren Schmitt

7 - Jeep B-11
Cpl. Robert Conrad
T/5 Eugene Garrett

8 - 2 1/2-ton Truck
T/5 Vester Wiles
Cpl. David Lucas
Pfc. Harry Horn

To
Ligneuville

N23

Farm Trail

DITCH

DITCH

DITCH

#10

© Kinunder 1993

BAUGNEZ-CK

the men said one looked like 2nd Lt. Solomon Goffman. When they arrived back at the crossroads, they saw quite a few from B Battery already in the field.

S/Sgt. William Merriken's story confirms many of the details of events at the front of the column. Capt. Mills, Lt. Lary, and their driver, Cpl. Raymond Lester, were in the lead jeep. Merriken was riding in the second vehicle, a two and one-half ton truck, with Pvt. Gilbert Pittman as driver, and Pfc. Aubrey Hardiman. All of them were sitting in the front of the truck. The convoy crossed the junction at Baugnez and continued forward. Merriken noticed that it was clear on both sides but the left side (east) sloped away from the road.

Moments later, the personnel in the jeep and truck noticed exploding shells in the field to the front and right of them. Lester suddenly pulled his jeep over to the right side of the road, closely followed by Pittman in the truck. They swerved and stopped as more shells came from the left and fell in the field to their right. Everyone got out of the truck and took cover in the ditch that ran beside the road on the right (west) side.

Minutes later, an American jeep with an officer and his driver drove out of the woods from the direction of Ligneuville into the battle and approached the head of the column. They slowed to a stop, but the men of B Battery yelled to them, "Keep going to Malmédy and get help." The jeep sped off toward Malmédy "going like hell!" This was the same jeep that later ran into the four vehicles coming from Malmédy trying to catch up with the convoy.

Immediately after the jeep roared off, Merriken ran across the road to the east side to see where the firing was coming from, then took cover in a ditch. He recalled seeing T/5 Albert Valenzi cross the road to get a better field of fire. About halfway across the road Valenzi fell, wounded in the leg. Ignoring his wound, Valenzi crawled the rest of the way across the road.

Merriken then glanced back toward the rear of the column and saw some B Battery vehicles stopped by the side of the road. His view of the rest of the convoy was obstructed by a bend in the road. Merriken pulled out his .45 pistol even though he knew it would be useless at such long range. He climbed a slight embankment to a wood pile to see if he could locate the enemy, but he could not. As he turned and started crawling back toward Valenzi, more German shells fell so he stopped and took cover in the ditch. The first shell ripped into the top of the fourth or fifth vehicle in the convoy. Panzer shells knocked over two other vehicles as the men hugged the ground. Debris from the knocked-out vehicles went flying around. Miraculously, after the shelling had subsided there did not appear to be any casualties.

Then the Americans heard the rumble of a tank coming around the bend in the road. All of them were hoping it was American, but as soon as it reached the bend, a "Kraut" standing in the turret fired the tank's machine gun at random. Lary yelled at the men to surrender as they began to rise from the ditches on both sides of the road. The German in the turret shouted "Up! Up! Up!" and motioned them toward the rear of the column.

Merriken stashed his pistol and holster in the woodpile and proceeded ahead of Lary's group on his way to the rear of the column. He heard one or two shots fired by the lead tank after he started walking. He thought that the Germans were firing at the officers in the lead vehicle, but he dared not turn around to see if anyone was hit.

A column of German vehicles filed past the Americans, heading south toward Ligneuville. As the Germans passed, they kept telling the Americans to keep moving. A German officer was standing up in his vehicle as he drove by. He looked directly at Merriken and in perfect English said, "It's a long way to Tipperary."

As Merriken and the others walked, there was a great deal of movement on the part of the Germans as they pushed the disabled American equipment over into the ditch or moved the vehicles to a point where they could be driven off. There was a constant stream of voices shouting and vehicles moving. Merriken was aware of men lying on the side of the road, conspicuously not moving. He did not know how many casualties there were.

As Merriken's group approached the rear of the column, he saw most of B Battery herded together in a field to the left (west). They were standing about fifty feet from the road facing it with their hands over their heads. At this point Merriken's group, the last group of POWs, was individually searched by two or three

Germans. "They took Merriken's watch and attempted to take his Bedford High School ring."[61] It was so cold and Merriken's fingers were so swollen that they could not get the ring off, so the German gave up and ordered Merriken into the field to join the rest of the Battery.

Sgt. Kenneth Ahrens was the observation sergeant in the Battery. He was near the front of the convoy with T/4 Albert Valenzi, T/5 Michael Skoda, and Cpl. Mike Sciranko. Their jeep was the third vehicle in the convoy. As soon as the firing started they dismounted and got into the ditch that ran along the west side of the highway. The ditch provided little protection, so they crawled across the road and found shelter behind house #10.

When the first panzer rounded the bend, the Germans motioned for the Americans to lay down their weapons and head back north toward the crossroads. Ahrens, Valenzi, and the rest of the Americans from the front of the column marched back toward the crossroad on both sides of the road. As they marched, the Germans asked them questions in perfect English. Could they drive the vehicles? Did they have any weapons on them? They also told the Americans to keep their hands in the air.

Valenzi and Ahrens were stopped by a German vehicle and a German officer took a bandoleer of ammunition from Valenzi's neck.[62] When they reached a point 300 yards from where they had started, the Germans searched them for watches, rings, billfolds, cigarettes, and anything else of value. However, the Germans did not search Ahrens at this time. Instead they sent him to another point where the Germans searched the Americans again. After this second search, the POWs went into the field.

Since the personnel in the front of the column were the last to be captured, they were also the last to go into the field and also nearest to the captors guarding them from the road.

A few of the men of B Battery had been killed in the opening fire and lay on or beside the road. The majority of B Battery, which had surrendered by this time, were being rounded up and moved north to the crossroads. One American walking north toward the field evidently did not have his hands up high enough because a German shot him three times in the back. Based on the position of the body when it was recovered and the autopsy report, this unfortunate soldier was Pvt. Peter Phillips.

At the rear of the column was the kitchen truck with the following personnel: T/4 Selmer Leu, cook; S/Sgt. John Osborne, Mess Sgt.; T/5 Charles R. Breon, cook; Pvt. Andrew Profanchick, cook; and Pfc. Howard E. Desch, driver. T/5 John O'Connell, route marker, and Pfc. Homer D. Ford, MP, were already at the crossroads. T/5 Charles Haines was driving a weapons carrier behind the kitchen truck with T/5 Harold Billow and T/5 Charles Reding, a recent replacement. Their job, retrieving the route markers, made them the last vehicle in the convoy.[63]

Pfc. Ralph Law was driving a two and one-half ton truck, third from the rear of the convoy, commanded by Sgt. Alfred Kinsman who was sitting beside him in the front of the truck. There were six men in the back of the truck, each carrying a carbine.[64]

When the firing began, Sgt. Kinsman ordered Pfc. Law to stop the truck and everyone to take cover. These men ran behind Café Bodarwe (house #6). They were joined by Ford, Billow, O'Connell, Haines, and the men from the kitchen truck. Ford saw that the line of prisoners was moving up the road toward the crossroads, and all at once he did not feel very safe behind Café Bodarwe. He looked around for a better hiding place. There was an outbuilding not far away, but it was across an open stretch of ground. Ford led the way and the fifteen to twenty men sprinted across the open area. They could see from the barn that most of the convoy stopped, but only four of the vehicles were visible. The men had been in the barn only ten or fifteen minutes when two Germans approached the barn with "burp guns." In broken English, they ordered the Americans to come out with their hands up. Outside the barn, they were searched for weapons. Henri Lejoly, the man in the Café with Madame Bodarwe, "had pointed them out to the Germans."[65]

Within a few minutes, these men, except Reding, were forced to join the POWs in the field. Reding crawled into some bushes on the north side of the Café Bodarwe (house #6) and was not discovered by the Germans. The remainder of the Battery was brought to the road junction where the Germans searched them and took their wrist watches and other valuables. An SPW stopped and a big fellow with an orange or yellow jacket stood up in this vehicle and said something. He motioned with his hands and almost immediately the POWs were herded into the field by some German soldiers with rifles. As they marched into the field, the Germans stayed on the road and two panzers stopped. The second panzer had a machine gun facing toward the field. Two Americans saw him load the weapon and one asked the fellow standing next to him what the Germans were going to do.

As the Germans gathered the POWs in the field, several members of B Battery were playing out their own fate at the southern end of the convoy near house #10, approximately 900 yards from the crossroads. They were T/5 Eugene Garrett, Pfc. Donald Bower, Cpl. Bob Conrad, Cpl. George Graeff, and T/5 Warren Schmitt. During the initial firing, they had made their way to a ditch which went off to the right (west) of N23 (see map page 51.)

During this time, "Schmitt submerged himself in the ditch and covered himself with weeds and whatever else he could find."[66] Conrad pretended to be dead; Graeff and Garrett were lying in the ditch on top of him. After approximately an hour, they tried to crawl out of the ditch but were so stiff they had to roll. They made their way to a firebreak in the woods.

Meanwhile, Pfc. Donald Bower jumped from his vehicle and made his way to a ditch west of the highway and played dead. After the first few vehicles in the German armored column passed by, Bower moved to another ditch fifteen yards west. Bower could hear the Germans looting the American vehicles and driving off several of the trucks. He also saw Lary and Hardiman marching north back toward the crossroads. At that time, Bower noticed four Germans with a machine gun in front of house #10 to his right.

About five minutes later Bower heard brush rustle in a ditch about fifteen yards away. Thinking they had sent a man out to get him, he said, "Kamerad" and came out and started walking toward the machine gun. He noticed Schmitt in the place where the brush was rustling. A German on a passing SPW whistled at Bower and pointed toward the German machine gun nest. When Bower, unarmed, started toward the road, a soldier in the SPW took three deliberately aimed shots at him. When one of the bullets sliced through his coat, he fell as if hit and played dead. As he fell, he spotted Garrett, Graeff, and Schmitt lying in the ditch near him.

George Graeff, Warren Schmitt, Donald Bower, Gene Garrett, and Robert Conrad escaped detection at the southern end of the convoy by hiding and playing dead. This picture was taken at the temporary monument in Baugnez (same site of permanent monument today) in August 1945.

T/5 Gene Garrett and T/4 Robert Mearig with other unidentified Americans standing at the Baugnez crossroads in the summer of 1945.

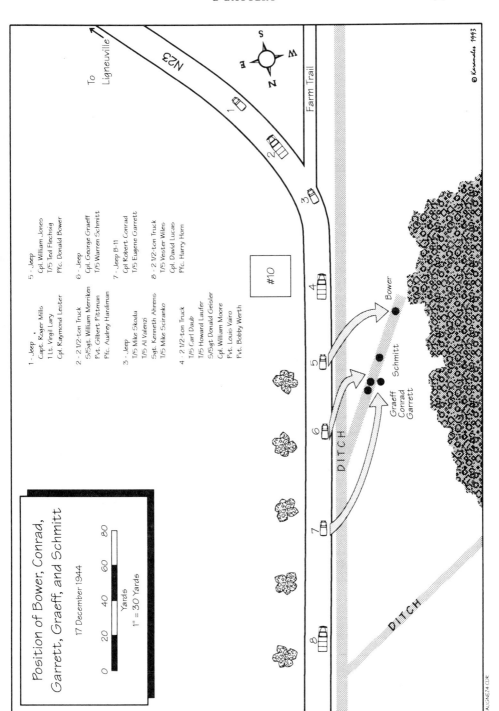

Position of Bower, Conrad, Garrett, Graeff, and Schmitt

17 December 1944

0 20 40 60 80
Yards
1" = 30 Yards

To
Ligneuville

N23

Farm Trail

© Kennedes 1993

DITCH

DITCH

#10

Bower

Schmitt

Graeff
Conrad
Garrett

1 - Jeep
Capt. Roger Mills
1 Lt. Virgil Lary
Cpl. Raymond Lester

2 - 2 1/2-ton Truck
S/Sgt. William Merriken
Pvt. Gilbert Pittman
Pfc. Audrey Hardiman

3 - Jeep
T/5 Mike Skoda
T/5 Al Valenzi
Sgt. Kenneth Ahrens
T/5 Mike Sciranko

4 - 2 1/2-ton Truck
T/5 Carl Daub
T/5 Howard Laufer
S/Sgt. Donald Geisler
Cpl. William Moore
Pvt. Louis Vairo
Pvt. Bobby Werth

5 - Jeep
Cpl William Jones
T/5 Ted Flechsig
Pfc. Donald Bower

6 - Jeep
Cpl. George Graeff
T/5 Warren Schmitt

7 - Jeep B-11
Cpl Robert Conrad
T/5 Eugene Garrett

8 - 2 1/2-ton Truck
T/5 Vester Wiles
Cpl. David Lucas
Pfc. Harry Horn

BALIGNE74 CDR

Graeff saw Bower get shot and fall down. He heard Garrett say, "They got Bower." During a short break in the movement of the Germans, Garrett said, "Let's go." As Graeff started to crawl, he reached back for Conrad but got no response. He reached down and moved Conrad's leg out from beneath him. Conrad responded and asked, "What happened?"[67]

Graeff told Conrad that they were leaving. These four men crawled to the edge of the woods to the west where they waited for Schmitt, but he never showed up. They went back and searched for him; but when they were unable to locate him, they headed northwest back toward Malmédy using the stars as a guide. Conrad was in bad shape from overexposure and shock, so they carried or supported him as he walked. They arrived in Malmédy after dark without further incident.

Schmitt was so cold from lying in the water-filled ditch for several hours he was unable to go with the others. After an SPW picked up the machine gun nest, things got quiet. Schmitt crawled slowly to the woods about twenty-five yards away and spent time getting the circulation back in his legs. He then walked to Malmédy, arriving late that night.

Several of the men behind the woodpile of house #10 saw four American soldiers run across the field from the road toward the woods. One of them made it to the woods, but Germans shot the others and they fell. Two German soldiers went over and made the two who had fallen near the edge of the woods get up and move back toward the road. On the way back, they came upon the other American soldier. He was wounded. They stopped and shot him with a pistol as he lay on the ground. (He could have been T/5 Wilson Jones, Jr., whose body was not found until April 1945.)

T/5 Kenneth Kingston was near the crossroads waiting for the Germans to decide what to do with the prisoners. Several hundred yards to the south, Kingston saw three or four Americans take off toward the west. These men did not have a chance and the Germans on the panzers shot them down. Only one man succeeded in getting away and it looked as if he was wounded.

It is possible that geography played a part in this atrocity and the fate of the prisoners. Armored policy forbade the panzers to stop and concern themselves with prisoners. This was left up to the men on foot, usually the panzer grenadiers (armored infantry) or, as happened in this case, the pioniers (engineers). If the Germans had moved the prisoners north from the crossroads, they would have walked into the lines of Lt. Col. Pergrin's 291st Engineers who controlled Malmédy. Going east on N32 toward Waimes, they would have eventually come in contact with the 99th Infantry Division lines. Moving south or west also would have brought them to American lines and safety for the prisoners.

The Germans had a dilemma as to what to do with their captives. Besides the location of the incident, there were several other factors which most likely contributed to the decision to massacre the prisoners. First, this particular group of Germans was the spearhead and had to move fast. Second, they were armored troops who were not supposed to deal with prisoners. Third, they had recently helped clean up cities that had been bombed by the Allies and had seen the terrible loss of civilian lives and the destruction on German soil. Fourth, they had recently committed smaller atrocities in Honsfeld and points east of Baugnez. These things had a persuasive effect on many of the members of the Kampfgruppe, especially the ones who were only seventeen and eighteen years of age. As a result, those left in charge probably either felt the most expedient thing to do was to "get rid of the POWs" or had orders to do so.

Seven men, even though they had a very difficult time, were fortunate not to be taken back to the atrocity field. The following soldiers escaped and did not suffer the horrors of their comrades: M/Sgt. Eugene Lacy, T/5 Tom Bacon, Cpl. David L. Lucas, T/5 Ralph Logan, together with three men from the 32nd Armored Regiment, 3rd Armored Division. Sgt. Vernon Anderson, Cpl. J. I. Cummings, and Pvt. William Barron were forced to drive the undamaged American vehicles for the Germans toward Ligneuville. Little did these men realize how lucky they were, although at the time they had no way of knowing what would happen to their comrades. All survived prisoner of war camps except Lucas who died March 3, 1945, at Stalag 4 near Dresden, Germany. According to the official German death certificate, he died from a weakness of the heart muscle.

Logan and Pfc. P. J. Martin were riding in a two and one-half ton truck with a trailer. Logan was driving for the Sound Platoon and was halfway back in the convoy. When the shelling started,

Logan stopped the truck and both men took cover in the ditch that ran along N23. As the Germans came down N23, they ordered Martin and Logan, with other Americans, to join a small group of prisoners already standing on the road. When Logan and Martin got to this group, they stood next to Valenzi who had been with the other prisoners sent back from the front of the column. The Germans asked if any of the prisoners could drive. Valenzi said that he could not drive and the German asking the question got extremely upset. Logan immediately volunteered to drive so the German would not shoot someone. The Germans ordered the drivers into the trucks and sent Martin, Valenzi, and the others toward the crossroads. Other than Bacon, who is discussed below, it is unknown how the other drivers were selected.

Bacon had kept Pfc. David Murray and Pfc. Carl Stevens with him, trying to get to a truck with a stretcher for Stevens. A German enlisted man came along motioning with his hands and saying, "Chauffeur," and Bacon thought he meant "stretcher" so the three started up the column with him. They reached a two and one-half ton truck, filled with five gallon gas cans. The German told Bacon to get in and drive. Then he motioned for Stevens and Murray to join the column going to the rear. The gas truck had been driven by T/4 Vester Wiles; but for some reason the Germans ordered him back to join the group at the crossroads. As Bacon climbed into the cab of Wiles' truck, he noticed one or two of the B Battery men who had been left in the ditch for dead.[68]

When the German column moved out to the south, Bacon drove the gas truck with them. After driving the truck about two miles toward Ligneuville, Bacon stopped because the Germans had become involved in a firefight with members of the 14th Tank Battalion and a few members from the 27th Armored Infantry Battalion. These troops had been surprised at Ligneuville by the Kampfgruppe. While this skirmish was going on, Bacon got the truck stuck by driving it into a ditch and he used the confusion as a means of escape. After escaping, he wandered around the area for about a week before being recaptured. He was moved to Germany where he spent the next six months in prisoner of war camps.[69] Bacon was sent to Stalag 6G near Bonn and from there transferred to Stalag 11B near Hanover. That POW camp was liberated by British troops in April 1945, and Bacon was flown to a hospital in England where he found out the fate of B Battery while reading *Life* magazine.

CHAPTER 5

INVOLVEMENT OF AMERICANS FROM OTHER UNITS

IN MANY ACCOUNTS of the Malmédy Massacre, B Battery of the 285th Field Artillery Observation Battalion was the only American unit involved. This chapter will show how several men from other units became victims of this atrocity.

Two medics, Pvt. Samuel Dobyns and Pfc. Wayne Scott, 575th Ambulance Company, had just left the 44th Evacuation Hospital at Malmédy. They worked their way into the 285th convoy as it moved south toward St. Vith. When Dobyns and Scott reached the crossroads at Baugnez, they turned east onto the road toward Waimes. They traveled approximately 600 yards east of the crossroads at Baugnez when a German panzer riddled their ambulance with machine gun bullets. Neither Dobyns nor Scott was wounded during this initial burst of fire; however, Scott lost control of the vehicle, and it crossed the road and ran into a field. At the time of the shooting, the ambulance plainly exhibited a Red Cross on the top, both sides, rear, and front. Dobyns and Scott immediately took cover in a ditch. The Germans ceased firing, and a German officer came over and relieved Dobyns and Scott of cigarettes and took a fountain pen from Scott. Dobyns and Scott climbed aboard a panzer and rode back to the crossroads at Baugnez.

About the same time Dobyns and Scott were captured, another ambulance came from the direction of Malmédy. T/5 Kenneth Kingston saw an ambulance pull up to the crossroads about the time he got to Café Bodarwe with the other prisoners from B Battery. Pvt. Keston Mullen from the 546th Ambulance Company drove the ambulance with T/5 Dayton Wusterbarth in command. A German panzer was already at the crossroads and it machine-gunned the ambulance.

A weapons carrier was the last vehicle in the 285th convoy. There were three more ambulances behind it and in front of Mullen and Wusterbarth. These ambulances were coming from the 44th Evacuation Hospital at Malmédy, heading east to the 47th Field Hospital at Waimes. In the ambulance directly behind the weapons carrier was Pfc. James McKinney and his assistant driver, Pfc. Stephen Domitrovich, from the 575th Ambulance Company. In the next two ambulances, also from the 575th Ambulance Company, were 1st Lt. Carl Genthner with his driver Pfc. Paul Paden; and, in the last ambulance, Pfc. L. M. Burney and Pvt. Roy Anderson. These ambulances had fallen in behind the weapons carrier and were about to turn east onto N32 heading toward Waimes when the firing started.

When McKinney and Domitrovich came up the hill with the other traffic, they heard a lot of shooting. They thought it was a plane "strafing." They stopped the ambulance, jumped into a ditch, and then crawled up a small hill to a barn attached to a Belgian farmhouse. This was house #7. A German officer and an enlisted man discovered McKinney and Domitrovich and searched them on the spot before sending them to join the other men in the field.

Three trucks from B Company, 86th Engineer Battalion (HP), were in the Malmédy area hauling lumber for pup tent flooring. As the trucks came up the hill from Malmédy toward Baugnez, they received small arms fire from one of the "SPWs" already there.

These vehicles stopped behind the last ambulance and all of the men in the logging trucks, except Pfc. John Clymire, jumped into the ditch on the west side of the road. He stayed in his truck and surrendered as the Germans came down the road in one of their SPWs, shooting up the logging trucks. Another man, Pvt. Vestal McKinney, received a bullet in the leg but was helped to safety by the other four men from B Company.

Two men, Sgt. Benjamin Lindt and Pfc. Elmer Wald, from the 200th Field Artillery Battalion had "MGP" on their helmets when their bodies were recovered. Men with this helmet marking performed police duties for the local population, such as enforcing curfew laws and performing various other civilian law enforcement duties in the occupied area. How those men became involved in the massacre is speculation; the best guess is that they encountered Kampfgruppe Peiper somewhere to the east of Baugnez before the massacre occurred. The only information available about them said, "They were Missing in Action from their unit as of December 18, 1944."[70] Their bodies were in the field with the others who died in the massacre.

Eleven soldiers from Reconnaissance Company, 32nd Armored Regiment, 3rd Armored Division, were involved in the massacre. They had left the vicinity of Stolburg, Germany, on patrol early in the morning of December 17, 1944. Normally recon jeeps carried three men: a driver, a radio operator, and a jeep commander. However, on this day the four jeeps contained only eleven men because the jeep in which Cpl. Walter Wendt was riding only had two men.

The men from this company were 1st Lt. Thomas McDermott, 2nd Lt. Lloyd Iames, Pfc. John Klukavy, T/3 James McGee, Sgt. Henry Zach, Sgt. Marvin Lewis, Sgt. Vernon Anderson, Pvt. William Barron, Cpl. Edward Bojarski, Cpl. J. I. Cummings, and Wendt. These men were on a reconnaissance mission heading south toward the vicinity of St. Vith.

In the jeep with Lt. Iames was Cummings, the driver, and Anderson in back as radio operator. According to Cummings "we had nothing to worry about."

The day was partly cloudy and occasionally the sun would peek through and they could see several P-51's diving and strafing.

T/3 James McGee of Reconnaissance Company, 32nd Armored Regiment, 3rd Armored Division shown on leave in the summer of 1944. He was KIA at Baugnez.

Courtesy of Francis W. Baker

As they rode along, everybody was talking and enjoying the winter scenery. Anderson said, "We must be close to the end of our mission." How right he was! They went through a little village and the people were out waving little American flags and smiling.

They moved along a fog-shrouded road and went down a slight hill. As they started up the other side, a high bank blocked the view ahead. At this moment the lead jeep almost ran into a German panzer which was moving slowly from the opposite direction. Before they could turn around in the narrow Belgian road, German infantry surrounded them. The Germans were hollering and screaming so much that it reminded Cummings of a cowboy and indian movie. They took the Americans by total surprise.

The Germans took the captured Americans up to the first panzer and began to question them. Cummings was standing on the left of Lt. McDermott when the German officer started to question him. Cummings stated that he was very scared because when a German officer would ask McDermott a question the Lt. would come right back with a smart answer. The German officer told McDermott that the Germans would be in Paris by tomorrow at this time. McDermott shot back that the only way that would happen would be if the Germans were the prisoners. The German officer came to Cummings and asked what division he was in, what their mission was and what the M.G.P. on the helmets stood for. Cummings only gave his name, rank and serial number.

According to Cummings, the German officer was very well dressed, slim and clean shaven. The German had graying temples, looked to be about forty years old and weighed between 160 and 170 lbs. He spoke very good English and told them he got his education near Boston. This officer motioned Cummings to place his jeep in the middle of the German column, and they started up and began moving west.

Between Schoppen and Ondenval (see map page 10), Kampf-gruppe Peiper turned west on a narrow, muddy farm trail. "Zach's jeep, which contained Lts. Iames and McDermott, burned out its clutch, so the three of them had to ride on the turret of the nearest panzer."[71]

While the colum stopped, someone sent a young German soldier to drive Cummings' jeep and at the same time placed Anderson and Barron in it. The column went a short distance and stopped again, and this time they put two American officers, a Lt. Col. and probably a Maj., in the jeep with Cummings, Anderson and Barron.

The column moved along a road until it came to a forest which was not very large. Open terrain came into view to the west when the column emerged from these woods. About 1000 yards away, across an open field, were some American trucks going through a crossroads, heading south. The tanks fired on the trucks.

By the time Cummings' vehicle got to the crossroads, several Americans were being put into a field. At this time fate intervened for Cummings, Anderson and Barron. As the men were about to be placed into this field, a shell exploded nearby. The young German floorboarded the jeep and they took off, almost throwing everybody out of the jeep. They headed south, and a few minutes later roared into Ligneuville where the Germans were engaged in heavy fighting with parts of the 27th Armored Infantry Bn. and 14th Tank Bn. From Ligneuville the Americans were sent to a prisoner of war camp where they remained until the end of the war.

S/Sgt. Herman Johnson and his assistant cook, Pvt. Edgar Smith, from M Company, 23rd Infantry Regiment, 2nd Infantry Division, were in a mess truck east of Waimes when the truck was hit by German artillery. Pvt. Smith was injured. Johnson put Smith into a jeep driven by Pvt. Wilson of Service Company, 23rd Infantry Regiment, for transport to an aid station. Going around a curve of a fog-shrouded highway about 8:30 A.M., Johnson, Smith, and Wilson met a German panzer and surrendered. Smith and Wilson stayed in the jeep and were released because Wilson had on a Red Cross brassard.

Johnson was placed in an SPW in the German column. He rode around the country as a prisoner of the Germans while they were cutting American lines of communication. This group of German vehicles was not a part of Peiper's main force. At 1:00 P.M., the SPW in which Johnson was riding drove west on N32 from Waimes to Malmédy and came to the road junction at Baugnez. This SPW, several other SPWs, and a German panzer joined the main German force that had captured B Battery. They took Johnson's watch, and sent him over to join the American prisoners, all of whom had been disarmed and were standing in the open field approximately twenty yards west of N23.[72]

CHAPTER 6

AMERICAN VERSION OF THE MASSACRE

A T 1:30 P.M. the Germans began assembling their prisoners approximately sixty to eighty yards from the crossroads on the west side of road N23. There would be 111 POWs in the total group.

The first group stood somewhat in formation, roughly six to eight rows deep. More captured Americans, who had hidden behind the barn just south of Café Bodarwe, came into the field about fifteen minutes later. This group also included the men from the kitchen truck and several men from the last vehicles in the 285th's convoy. Homer Ford, the MP, and T/5 John O'Connell, the route marker from B Battery, were the last two in the group.

At the same time, medics Pfc. James McKinney, Pfc. Stephen Domitrovich, Pvt. Keston Mullen, T/5 Dayton Wusterbarth, Pvt. Roy Anderson, Pfc. L. M. Burney, and 1st Lt. Carl Genthner, who had been captured north of the crossroads, moved into the field. Also in this group was Pfc. John Clymire, from the B Company, 86th Engineer Battalion (HP). The last prisoners who came into the field were the men from the front of the 285th's convoy.

According to S/Sgt. William Merriken, B Battery, 285th Field Artillery, Observation Battalion, the following events preceded the massacre. As the last Americans climbed the fence and entered the field, there was a German (probably an officer) standing in an "SPW" on the extreme left (north) of the POW formation. On the right (south) of the group of the captives was also another SPW, with a manned machine gun. Merriken felt that the Germans were waiting for their trucks to come pick up the Americans to take them to Germany.

The weather was bitterly cold, overcast, around 32°F with extremely low clouds. Skiffs of snow and half frozen bits of water lay on the ground. Merriken had no gloves on and wore a jacket instead of a top coat. His arms were aching from holding his hands over his head so long. He began to get suspicious of an SPW on the road as he watched it move and try to lower its cannon on the POWs at close range. At that very moment, he thought, "They're going to slaughter us all with the cannon!" The SPW had trouble jockeying the cannon into a position to cover the POWs, gave up, and drove away to the south.

Merriken recalls feeling chill bumps go up and down his body when he saw the German standing in the vehicle on the left raise his pistol, take slow deliberate aim, and fire at the group. Merriken remembers the German firing at least three shots. He saw that the first victim was an officer, but did not believe he was from the 285th. Suddenly, the Germans in the two SPWs started yelling and firing machine guns at the prisoners. Merriken spun around and fell flat on the ground. His head turned to the left and his left arm covered his face. Immediately after he fell to the ground he was hit twice in the back by machine gun fire. The bullets lodged within inches of his spinal column. He could not see what was happening but could hear the agonized screams from those that had been hit, mixed with the constant chattering of the machine guns and the thuds of the bullets striking American bodies and the ground around him. Merriken says he has no idea how long the machine guns fired; it seemed like hours, but he is sure it was only minutes.[73]

Exactly what or who started the firing will never be known, but most accept the German statements as the truth. The Germans said that Sturmmann (Pfc.) George Fleps fired two shots at the southern end of the POWs as his panzer was moving slowly through the area. Based upon the time that Fleps arrived at the southern end of the field, he could have been firing at one or two of the Americans as they tried to escape westward. These men were probably from the group from the front of the convoy. Many of these men were placed in the southernmost section of the prisoners.

Cpl. Lester, driver for Capt. Mills and Lt. Lary, supposedly was the first man shot. However, since Lester's body was not found in the field with the other bodies, this seems unlikely. Many American statements claim that a medical officer, probably 1st Lt. Carl Genthner of the 575th Ambulance Company, was the first man shot. Seventy percent of the survivors said that a German, probably an officer, standing in an SPW or command car located on the road at the north end of the POWs, fired the first shot. This officer could have been one of several officers of Kampfgruppe Peiper, possibly even Hauptsturmführer (Capt.) Hans Gruhle, Adjutant of the Kampfgruppe.

After the initial two or three shots, the prisoners, with hands raised or clasped behind their heads, naturally started to run. Hoping to prevent further firing, 1st Lt. John Munzinger of B Battery, shouted "Stand fast!" However, the panzer and SPW machine guns opened fire at this point, sweeping the field from one end to the other. The time was about 2:20 P.M., December 17, 1944. This moment marked the approximate time of the first firing by the Germans.

All or most of the prisoners dropped to the ground and stayed there while this firing continued for about two to three minutes, wounding many of them. Men who had critical wounds thrashed about and moaned such things as "Mom" or "Oh, God." When the firing stopped, ten to twenty members from the 2nd Platoon, 3rd SS Panzer Pioneer Company, and some members of the Penal (Disciplinary) Platoon of the 9th SS Panzer Pioneer Company went into the field to kill the men still alive, or as the Germans say "to give mercy shots."

When the shooting stopped, T/5 Carl Daub, of B Battery, heard the Germans walking around the prostrate bodies. He had his face in the mud and thought they were looking to see if any of the

Americans were alive. Now and then he would hear them say something in German and then there would be the crack of small arms fire.[74]

Pfc. Aubrey Hardiman lay next to 1st Lt. Carl Genthner, 575th Ambulance Company, who was wounded in the first volley of shots. When the pioniers came into the field, Genthner said something to them in German, and they shot him three times. One of the bullets went through him and wounded Hardiman in the foot.[75]

Pvt. Donald Day fell face down in the back row facing the road, in the left corner of the field. He could not see anything after he fell but heard panzers coming by on the road. Each panzer that passed shot at the Americans. After the panzers went by, the Germans stood on the road and fired at anyone who moved or groaned. Then they came around through the field to Day's right, and continued to shoot anyone who moved. After that, things were quiet.[76]

Pfc. Ralph Law hit the ground when he realized the Germans were firing at him. A bullet hit him in the left leg as he lay in the field. The leg pained him at first; but after a couple of minutes it became numb. He lay there with his head down in a small patch of snow, not daring to move. He was conscious of someone walking among the wounded lying on the ground. One man close to him was hollering with pain. Law heard a shot close by, then the man was quiet.

Sgt. Ken Ahrens climbed through the fence surrounding the field. He noticed several men that did not belong to B Battery and also some aid men. One in particular, whose name was Cpl. Ralph J. Indelicato, was administering aid to a man from B Battery who had received a piece of shrapnel in the leg. Indelicato was wearing the Red Cross with a white background on all four sides of his helmet. He also had the Red Cross band on his left arm.

Ahrens also noticed a group of B Battery officers standing there in the group of prisoners who had congregated to the right of Ahrens. He wandered over into the left side of the group facing the road. He noticed practically all the members of his battery as they were grouped, approximately six to eight rows deep. He was standing along with T/5 Mike Skoda at the left side of the group in approximately the second or third line.

While they were standing there with their hands in the air, a tracked vehicle pulled up on the road about twenty yards from the prisoners. An officer or a non-com was standing on top of this vehicle. There were also a couple of other German tracked vehicles in front of the first vehicle. The German who was standing pulled out his pistol and took deliberate aim. It looked as if he were taking target practice as he fired into the unarmed prisoners. After the first shot Ahrens noticed a man from his battery drop to the ground, shot through the head. He was about ten feet away from Ahrens. By the time he looked back at the German, Ahrens heard another shot.

Immediately after the first two shots rang out, the machine guns opened up on the prisoners. Ahrens spun around and fell face first on the ground. As he lay there, several bullets hit him in the back. The Germans then came into the field and shot anyone who was breathing, moaning, or praying. Ahrens heard various thuds as the Germans kicked the men to find out who was alive. These Germans shot approximately forty of the POWs through the head at point blank range.

Ahrens saw these Germans laughing and having a very good time with their killing. Only a few feet away, he watched as the medic, Indelicato, unable to bear the sounds of pain from a man beside him, raised up on one knee and took his first-aid kit from his pocket and plugged Pfc. Carl Stevens' bullet hole with a wad of bandage. Indelicato evidently believed the Red Cross on his helmet would be honored. Ahrens watched in horror as a pionier walked over and stood beside Indelicato, waited for him to finish the bandaging, then shot both men. Another pionier walked over and the two Germans turned around, laughing together. These two Germans walked toward Ahrens, and he thought his time had come. He breathed as lightly as he could. "Tot" (dead), they said, and walked on. Ahrens guessed that the wound in his back had soaked the uniform with so much blood it was easy to believe that he was dead. A man lying next to Ahrens had been alive until a bullet pierced his stomach. They had been whispering and praying just before the fateful shot. Later, when Ahrens got up to run, he kicked the man and told him to come on but there was no response.[77]

T/5 Charles Appman recalled one soldier with a steel helmet and a dark uniform pointing a pistol and firing into the crowd. A fellow standing to Appman's left fell over. The man with the pistol laughed and again raised the pistol. The German fired the second time and Appman heard someone to his right rear fall. Almost immediately a man with a machine gun opened fire upon the group of prisoners. Appman made a half turn to the right and dove for the ground. He lay there between two other soldiers and kept as still as he could. A few minutes later the machine gunning stopped and he heard some German soldiers walking among the wounded. He could hear many POWs moaning. Periodically, he would hear someone speaking German and then a pistol shot. The pioniers searched among the bodies for about fifteen minutes, and then they returned to the road. As Appman lay there he heard the Germans mount the vehicles and continue down the road. As they left, they fired into the men lying in the field.[78]

T/5 Ted Paluch saw an SPW that took up a diagonal position and pointed its cannon at the Americans. It soon backed into the road and moved on southward. Shortly thereafter he watched as a German vehicle, something like a jeep, came down the road from the intersection. As it headed south, a German in the vehicle took two shots at the POWs with a pistol. These two shots hit one fellow on Paluch's left and one on his right. Everybody in the field fell flat to the ground at the second shot. This vehicle, from which the first two shots came, was moving slowly at the time. As far as Paluch knew, it continued down the road.

As the afternoon progressed, Paluch could hear panzers and SPWs round the corner at the crossroads and head south. As each vehicle neared the field, it opened up with its machine gun on the Americans lying in the field. The firing ceased after the vehicle passed the field. It would not commence again until another vehicle had rounded the corner and started down the road. Paluch had a bullet graze the little finger of his right hand.

During a break in the column, Paluch heard the voices and footsteps of what he believed were three German soldiers walking in the field where the men lay, shooting anyone who showed any sign of life. They did not shoot at Paluch. After this happened, more vehicles came around the corner, continued down the road, and fired at the POWs as they went by.[79]

Corporal Wendt of Reconnaissance Company, 32nd Armored Regiment, stated later, "I heard the Germans say 'Da kriegt noch einer Luft,' meaning 'There's one still breathing,' and then there would be a shot."[80]

Pfc. Mario "Boots" Butera lay on the ground for about five minutes until the firing ceased, feigning death. Butera was conscious as he lay there and could hear Germans talking and laughing. A German approached one of his companions who was lying beside Butera moaning and spitting blood. This German fired four pistol shots into Butera's friend.[81]

T/5 Kenneth Kingston was a very fortunate soldier. As he lay in the field a German reached for Kingston's watch. As the German was attempting to get the watch from Kingston's wrist, he felt Kingston's pulse. The German immediately pulled out his pistol and pointed it at Kingston's head. At exactly the moment the German pulled the trigger, one of his friends called to him. He turned just enough to cause the bullet to barely miss Kingston's head, as it entered his helmet.

After spending about fifteen minutes in the field, the pioniers went back to their vehicles and moved southward as the main body of Kampfgruppe Peiper approached from the direction of Waimes. As these vehicles came opposite the field in which the prisoners were lying, some also aimed small arms fire and machine guns at the prostrate bodies. This intermittent firing continued for the next hour or so — the time it took for the main body of the Kampfgruppe to pass.

CHAPTER 7

THE ESCAPES

F OR A TIME after the massacre, those who were still alive lay quietly on the ground. After the last vehicles of Kampfgruppe Peiper passed the field, things became quiet for a few minutes but the survivors could still hear some German voices and noises coming from a panzer having mechanical problems on the road to Waimes. About 4:00 P.M., one of the Americans said, "Let's make a break for it," or words to that effect. Some attribute this statement to Pvt. Jim Mattera, others to Pvt. William Reem or Pfc. Ralph Law. Most of those still alive got up and ran in a north-westerly direction toward Malmédy; even those seriously wounded tried to get away.

Pvt. John Kailer and Pfc. Carl Frey ran with eight to ten other men northwest across a dirt road, and toward some woods. The Germans still had a panzer (#114) near the crossroads, and it fired its machine gun at the group. When the Germans started firing, both Kailer and Frey hit the ground, with Frey landing about five feet in front of Kailer. Frey was about six feet from the road to Hedomont. The Germans were still firing the machine gun from the panzer when one of the crew came up the road with a pistol and commenced shooting everybody he saw. Kailer, lying partially on his left side with his right arm in front of his face, saw this German run up the road and shoot Pvt. Samuel Hallman of B Battery who was lying behind Kailer. The German then aimed at Kailer and fired. Kailer felt the bullet graze his right forearm, and he watched as the German shot Frey (see map page 106).

About five to ten minutes later, Kailer, still lying on the ground, heard two more Germans coming up the road through the field. They were kicking the bodies, and Kailer could hear the men grunt. After kicking a POW, the Germans would either shoot him or go on to the next man. They got to Hallman and kicked him three times, cursing when he grunted. They shot him and continued across the road. For some unknown reason they did not come up to Kailer. Instead, they cut across the dirt road heading north through the field. There must have been other prisoners in that area because he saw the Germans stop and heard shots from that direction. Kailer was about 150 yards west of the crossroads, and very close to the hedgerow that bordered the road to Hedomont.[82]

S/Sgt. William Merriken, who was wounded in the back and right leg, took the same path as Kailer. Merriken was probably shot at by the same German who shot at Kailer and shot Pvt. Samuel Hallman (#58), Pfc. Carl Frey (#59), and T/5 Robert McKinney (#60) (see map page 106). Another German was running up the road to Hedomont after the escaping Americans. He spotted Merriken struggling to get over the fence that bordered this road. He aimed at Merriken and fired from a few yards away; luckily the pistol did not fire and the German kept running toward the other escaping men. This German probably figured he would get Merriken on the way back since Merriken was already severely wounded.

On the opposite side of the road was a shed behind a Belgian farmhouse (house #7). Merriken threw himself at a fence that ran alongside the road to Hedomont. This fence, like many Belgian fences, was made up of a hedge-like bush. Merriken crashed through, landed in the ditch on the other side, and crawled across the road to the shed. He watched from the shelter of the shed as the German came back down the road. Merriken was in pain and weak from loss of blood. Shortly thereafter, he fell asleep.

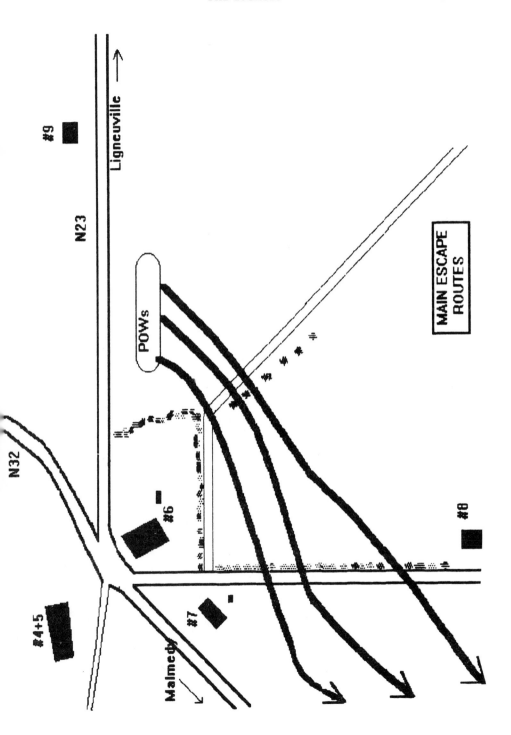

This is the shed where S/Sgt. William Merriken and T/5 Charles Reding hid for several hours on the night of 17 December 1944. Early the next morning they left the shed and were found by a Belgian couple who hid them for several days.

Courtesy of William Merriken

When the survivors returned to the scene of the atrocity in the summer of 1945, this is how the shed appeared.

Courtesy of William Merriken

When Merriken awoke and looked between the shed's slats, he saw a man crawling along the edge of the road on the opposite side, heading across the road toward the shed. Merriken was unsure whether the wounded man was American, so he armed himself with a large piece of wood he found in the woodshed, determined not to be killed without a fight.

The man turned out to be T/5 Charles "Chuck" Reding, a recent replacement to B Battery. He had been riding in the weapons carrier which was the last vehicle in the convoy. This lucky young soldier had crawled into some brush on the north side of Café Bodarwe after the shelling and was not captured by the Germans. He stayed there until nightfall, crawled up the road westward, turned north, and met Merriken in the shed by accident.

Immediately, Merriken and Reding began to think of how to get out of the area and back to Malmédy. In the early morning of December 18, they crawled out of the woodshed and down toward N23. They turned and went parallel to N23 to avoid being spotted by the Germans at the crossroads. Merriken's wounds caused the men to make limited progress and they had to stop and rest many times. They finally found a thicket near the village of Geromont, halfway between Malmédy and Baugnez, where they spent the night of the 18th. Merriken's wounds became unbearable. A Belgian civilian spotted the two Americans and motioned them toward Geromont. There a Belgian couple assisted the men for two days by giving them first aid and food. The lady then went to Malmédy to get help for Merriken and she returned with medics who took Merriken and Reding back to the hospital in Malmédy. Much later, as Merriken was being loaded into an ambulance, Reding came by to see him off. They parted with the words, "Goodbye good buddy."[83]

A few of the men waited in the field until dark and made their escape under the cover of night, including Pvt. Harry Horn from B Battery. Horn ran with the others; but because of his stomach wounds, he fell approximately seventy to eighty yards from the massacre site. Later he watched two Germans come into the field to loot the bodies. Horn, badly wounded, left the area after dark, crossing northeast of the crossroads where a Belgian family found him. They cared for him for four days, washed his wounds, and gave him food and cognac. Horn stayed with this family until aid men from the 99th (Norwegian) Infantry Battalion picked him up.

Another survivor who waited until nightfall was S/Sgt. Henry Zach of the Reconnaissance Company, 32nd Armored Regiment, 3rd Armored Division. Zach was wounded in the hip during the initial firing and was shot the second time in his left thigh by a pionier who came into the field to give "mercy shots." Zach wrote to the author in June 1992 and described his escape.

> As I was lying in the field a medic suddenly appeared and began treating a wounded American just to my southwest. As he left he said he would get some help but just a few minutes later I heard some pistol shots from the area of the crossroads and I figured he had run into trouble. I waited awhile longer and saw two Americans rise up from the pile of dead and wounded bodies. They began staggering and weaving, holding each other up as they made their way out of the field heading toward the crossroads.
>
> I waited awhile longer, til it was completely dark, and hearing no more shots I sat up. By pushing with my right leg and using both arms, I slowly made my way toward the building (café) at the crossroads. When I got there I pulled some of the debris over me and fell asleep. The next day when I heard voices I crawled out from my hiding place. Friendly or not I knew that I was about done if I didn't get some help for my wounds. I was rescued by a medical officer and some of his men.

About 10:30 A.M. the morning after the massacre, Capt. Edward Schenk of the 955th Field Artillery Battalion arrived at Baugnez in a command car on his way from Butgenbach to Malmédy. With him were Sgt. Garn and driver T/5 Lieber. As Capt. Schenk slowly drove through the Baugnez crossroads area, civilians nearby beckoned frantically, and he went to investigate. They told Schenk that on the previous day many German panzers had come through the area and caught the Americans at this crossroads. The civilians asked him to come with them to a nearby house where they were taking care of two wounded American soldiers who they claimed were the only living Americans in the area. As Schenk started toward the house, Lieber, who had been looking around the area, suddenly called Schenk's attention to a cry of, "Help."

They immediately investigated and found Zach, severely wounded in his left leg below the knee and in his hip. He was conscious, so Schenk administered first aid and, with the assistance of Garn and Lieber, placed Zach in the command car. Zach was in such bad condition that Schenk told the civilians to continue to care for the other two wounded men, and he would send someone back later to pick them up.[84]

As T/5 Charles Appman lay in the field he heard someone say, "Let's go." He heard a commotion, got up, and saw about eight American soldiers making a dash for freedom. A German soldier who was still on the road hollered "Halt!" The Germans then fired a machine gun at the running Americans. Appman and another fellow crossed the road to Hedomont and ran down through a small valley. They ran to a house where they met a captain and an enlisted man from the 291st Engineer Battalion (probably Capt. John Conlin). The captain took them and two other men to the hospital at Malmédy.

Pfc. Ralph Law, who was shot in the leg early in the first German volley, saw the first group get up and run. Even though he was wounded, he decided to go, too. He jumped up and said, "Let's go," loud enough so that anyone that was still alive could hear him. Several men raised their heads and attempted to get up. It was everyone for himself to get out of there as the panzer at the crossroads opened fire at the escaping Americans. Four or five of the men were fairly close together as they crossed the field and started across the road to Hedomont. As Law started across, a German at the crossroads opened up with a "burp gun" from about fifty yards away. Law dropped into the ditch beside the road for cover; his leg hurt him too much to continue. The German with the "burp gun" ran up the road past Law, still shooting at the others running west. After the panzer stopped shooting, the German came back to Law who was lying on his face. The German kicked Law in the back to see if he was dead. Law held his breath for a very long time and the German, finally satisfied, continued back to his panzer at the crossroads. Law turned his head just enough to see the German as he got to the panzer.

The Germans in the panzer (#114) set fire to the barn, which later spread to the café. The light from the fire shone so brightly that Law had to lie in the ditch until the fire died down. It was about 11:00 P.M. before Law thought it was dark enough to safely leave the area. His leg was so stiff he could not bend it, but the wound had stopped bleeding.

Law turned around and crawled west up the ditch away from the crossroads. After about fifty yards, he went through the hedgerow into a field and crawled about a mile and a half across several fields. As day was breaking, he knew he had to seek cover so the Germans would not find him. Law crawled up to the back of a farmhouse and into the basement, which was at ground level. Law rattled the door, hoping it might be an American outpost, but the place was empty. Most of Law's clothes were soaking wet from crawling through the fields, and he was cold. He pulled off his overcoat and his leggings and threw them into a corner. He then lay on some old quilts he found in a corner.

As he got warm, he felt better and tried to figure some way to get out of there and get some help. Law raised up and saw a bicycle and a dry jacket. He put on the jacket and managed to get the bicycle out to the road. No one was in sight. By holding on to a small tree, he got on the bike. His left leg was too stiff and sore to be of any use, but the road was mostly downgrade and hard-surfaced so he coasted along for about a mile and a half.[85]

As Law approached a town, he was stopped by American infantrymen who were defending the town. A guard asked him who he was, and Law replied that he was a wounded American. They sent him along, still on the bicycle, to two medics about twenty-five yards farther on. The medics put him in a jeep and took him to an aid station. From there, Law was sent to a hospital near Liege.

Pvt. R. L. Smith was lying next to Pvt. William Reem who was giving an account of what was going on since he could see the entire area. These two men lay in the field for over an hour until one of the fellows who was lying nearby made a break. Everyone who could got up at that time. However, Smith's escape was slowed because his legs were numb from the cold, and by the time he got out of the field, the others were out of sight. As the circulation returned to Smith's legs, he went through a barbed wire fence, across a dirt road, and through a hedge and another barbed wire fence. Someone hollered behind him; it was Pvt.

Donald Day who was wounded in the leg. Smith waited for him. About that time, the Germans started shooting a machine gun at them from a panzer east of the crossroads. As the bullets kicked up the ground around them, they tried to run as best they could in their wounded condition. They limped away to the northwest and headed down through some woods toward Malmédy.

Smith and Day reached a railroad track and Day stopped a Belgian boy and asked him if he knew where there were any Americans. The boy said there were some on the highway ahead. They continued on and found two medics who flagged a jeep, which took Day and Smith to the 77th General Hospital. They put Day in the operating room right away and put Smith upstairs. Smith stayed there for three days until they shipped him back to the 76th General Hospital, then to a hospital in Paris, but he did not remember which one. He stayed there for about ten days, and then was returned to the 285th.[86]

Cpls. George Fox and Ted Flechsig ran in a northwest direction until they came to the road heading west to Hedomont. They turned west and ran and crawled to the crest of the hill west of the massacre site. Luckily, they found a bicycle. Flechsig rode since he was injured and Fox walked alongside and helped to keep Flechsig from falling. They continued until they came to a 291st Engineer Battalion roadblock near Stavelot, about five miles away.

T/5 Ted Paluch headed northwest, crossed a farm lane, and continued across a farm field and the road to Hedomont. He was shot at by a German, who missed, near the crossroads. Paluch fell down as he crossed the hedgerow on the north side of the road to Hedomont and played dead. He was about 100 yards from the crossroads at this time. The German who had shot at him came up the road, was apparently satisfied that Paluch was dead, and went back to the crossroads. After dark, Paluch made his way west to another hedgerow where he joined up with S/Sgt. Herman Johnson from the 2nd Infantry Division. As they were making their way back to Malmédy, they met one of the medics from the 575th, possibly Pvt. Roy Anderson.

Right after Paluch's group ran into the medic, they also came across Pvt. Jim Mattera of B Battery. Mattera had run in a northwest direction over a hill and down toward Malmédy. This group finally came upon one of the 291st roadblocks. "Forget the password!" Mattera shouted, "I'm from Lancaster County, Pennsylvania . . . outfit wiped out . . . the Germans are coming!"[87]

T/5 Kenneth Kingston, Pvt. William Reem, Pfc. Andrew Profanchick, and Sgt. Charles E. Smith headed north across open country and then ran down a valley. During their escape, the Germans fired at them with machine guns, but they eventually made their way back into Malmédy.

Pfc. Homer Ford, the MP at the crossroads, ran across the fields until he came to a secondary road which led him to Malmédy.

Cpl. Edward Bojarski, 32nd Armored Regiment, ran with five other men in a northwest direction, where they were later found by medics in a jeep and taken to Malmédy.

T/5 William Summers, T/5 Carl Moucheron, and Pfc. Mario Butera ran behind Café Bodarwe and crossed the road to Hedomont. They ran down the hill until they came to Malmédy, about two miles away.

Lt. Virgil Lary ran into the woods northwest of the field and hid until dark. He struck off cross-country toward Malmédy and entered the village of Floriheid, a mile southwest of Malmédy, about 11:00 P.M. He approached the Martin farmhouse to see if he could get help with his wounds. When he knocked on the door, Monsieur Martin and his two daughters helped Lary inside, performed first aid, and made him as comfortable as they could. Although Mon. Martin knew it was dangerous to be out in a combat area, he went to Malmédy to get help. After an hour he returned without help. Lt. Lary then insisted that he be taken to Malmédy even though his foot wound was severe. With the help of the Martin sisters and a makeshift crutch, Lary made his way to Malmédy, arriving there sometime in the early morning hours of December 18.

Pfc. Stephen Domitrovich, 575th Ambulance Company, ran with a large group back toward Malmédy. That was probably the large group that Bojarski ran with.

Sgt. Ken Ahrens, Cpl. Mike Sciranko, T/5 Al Valenzi, and T/5 Paul Gartska went across the road to Hedomont and ran until they ran into Lt. Col. David Pergrin, 291st Engineer Battalion, who was in command of the American forces in Malmédy. Pergrin and his driver had gone out to the crossroads to see what the firing was about.

Pfc. Aubrey Hardiman and T/5 Carl Daub got up and ran at the same time. They were leading a group of escapees, and Hardiman remembers stopping and taking off his overshoes so that he could move faster. He later bumped into a Belgian child who pointed the way to Malmédy.

T/5 John O'Connell ran with Pvt. Bobby Werth and Pvt. Samuel Dobyns, 575th Ambulance Company, in a northwest direction until they came to some woods. O'Connell was wounded in the jaw and thought that without medical aid he might die. He proposed to the others that he proceed down the road until he found help. He figured if he ran into the Germans, he would get medical treatment and if he ran into our forces, he would send help back to pick up Werth and Dobyns. He came into one of the 291st roadblocks and after sending men back for Werth and Dobyns, he was taken into the aid station in Malmédy.

S/Sgt. Herman Johnson, 2nd Division, ran in a northwest direction and found a barn where he hid until dark. Then he met with T/5 Paluch (see Paluch's story). They made it safely back to Malmédy.

T/4 Robert Mearig wandered around west of the area for several days prior to being picked up by American forces. Ironically, the man who found him was from his home town.

T/5 Harold Billow ran in a northwest direction and, when he got near the café, decided to go inside. From there he saw a German panzer sitting on the other side of the road. He immediately turned around, left the same way he entered, and went west along the road to Hedomont. He eventually made his way into Malmédy.

Perhaps the most bizarre escape belonged to T/5 Mike Skoda. Pfc. P. J. Martin, one of Skoda's buddies who had also played dead, was giving Skoda an eyewitness account of what was happening. Martin asked Skoda if he was hit. Skoda replied that he was hit in the shoulder but felt pretty good. When Skoda discovered that he could move his legs, they decided to make a run for it. The Germans started firing at them as they ran to a house about 350 yards up the road. They circled the building but could not get inside. They were able to enter the barn. Skoda wanted to stay because he was wounded. Martin thought they should move on because the barn was too close to the crossroad. Skoda was bleeding so he stayed in the barn while Martin crawled about 200 yards to a bend in the road. From there he walked across the fields to Malmédy where he was taken to the 67th Field Hospital.

Skoda saw a ladder that led to a trap door to the hayloft. He climbed up and covered himself with hay. Then he started taking account of where he was hit. He counted five holes in his shoulder so he took an old scarf from around his neck and wrapped his wounds. After that he passed out.

He stayed in the hayloft for four days without food or water except for a few drops from the ceiling of the barn. His feet were frost-bitten. After four days, Skoda left the barn to get some water out of a watering trough. He was so thirsty he pushed a cow out of the way so he could drink. While Skoda was drinking, a German came up and pointed a gun at Skoda's head. The German helped Skoda with his injuries before taking him to the German headquarters for questioning. Skoda did not want to admit he had witnessed the shooting at the crossroads so he did not tell them he had been part of it.

Following interrogation, Skoda was taken to Bonn, Germany, where he was kept in the choir loft of a chapel with thirty other prisoners. He did not get medical attention until December 27, because wounded Germans were given top priority. The German doctor who operated on Skoda had been educated in American schools and spoke fluent English. The doctor told Skoda he was amazed at how clean the wounds were. He thought Skoda should have been dead or at least have gangrene. The doctor removed all but one bullet which was lodged in Skoda's upper arm. If he had removed the last bullet, Skoda possibly would have lost the use of his left arm. (This bullet stayed with Skoda until he died in 1988.) After the operation, Skoda went back to the choir loft, and from there was taken to prison camp, Stalag 2B, Luckenwalde, near the Polish border.

He arrived at Stalag 2B and after only three or four days he became very ill. His temperature was up around 103° and the German hospital staff could not bring it down. The Germans brought in an Italian doctor who said Skoda had to be moved if he was to survive. Luckily, Skoda was able to exchange places with another prisoner who was being kept in isolation. He stayed in isolation for a week, and his temperature went back to normal.

Skoda was still at Stalag 2B in February when the Russians were moving forward with their offensive. The Germans were forced to evacuate and attempted to move the prisoners farther inside Germany. They left behind a small group of prisoners who could not walk. Skoda was among the group left behind because he continued to have problems with his feet.

This group was hiding in the potato cellar of Stalag 2B. A German soldier came down about 2:00 A.M. and asked if there were any Americans in the cellar. (There were only American prisoners left at the time.) They all spoke up, laughing, because they thought there was no way out. They thought the Germans were trapped, but they had forgotten about a canal that was nearby.

Skoda and the other Americans were taken via the canal to Potsdam, just outside of Berlin. They were held there until the Germans were forced to evacuate once again because of the Russian advance, this time leaving all their prisoners behind.

When the Russians came, they needed an interpreter. They were getting $10 for every American soldier they liberated and needed a list of names. Skoda spoke fluent Russian because his parents were Russian immigrants. As an interpreter, he was given special privileges. In fact, he was the only one permitted outside the camp. One Sunday afternoon, as he was walking outside the prison grounds, Skoda spotted an American jeep and hitched a ride out of Germany.[88]

CHAPTER 8

RECOVERY OF THE BODIES

THE INSPECTOR GENERAL'S OFFICE at the 1st U.S. Army Headquarters in Spa, Belgium, learned of the shootings three or four hours after the massacre. By the late evening of December 17, 1944 the rumor that the enemy was killing prisoners had reached as far as the forward American divisions. There were American commanders who expressed the opinion that all SS troops should be killed on sight and there was some indication that in isolated cases such orders were given. An order issued by Headquarters, 328th Infantry, on December 21 for the attack scheduled for the following day said, "No SS troops or paratroopers will be taken prisoners but will be shot on sight."[89]

Although the Americans were aware of the atrocity at Baugnez, they did not recapture that area until January 13, 1945. Several witnesses stated that many dead American soldiers were in the field southwest of the Baugnez crossroads. This was corroborated by the survivors' statements. The Germans had reinforced the area and brought the crossroads and the massacre field under artillery observation and fields of fire from machine guns. On January 3, 1945, B Company, 526th Armored Infantry Battalion, made several attempts to secure this area. Due to the entrenched

Germans and the heavy concentration of artillery fire, the Americans were repulsed with heavy casualties.

Officers from the Office of the Inspector General made repeated attempts to visit the scene of the atrocity, but the area remained in enemy hands. At 8:00 A.M. on January 13, 1945, the 120th Infantry Regiment, 30th Infantry Division, attacked. An infantry battalion attacked on each side of the crossroad, and at 11:00 A.M. a small reconnaissance party attempted to get to the area of the massacre. They started from Geromont, about a half mile north of Baugnez. About two feet of fresh snow had fallen throughout the area and the road was almost impassable, even for a jeep. On the way to the crossroads, the reconnaissance party encountered enemy sniper, machine gun, artillery, and small arms fire. The forward elements of the party reached the crossroads at approximately 1:00 P.M. and managed to crawl to the edge of the massacre field. A signal corps photographer took pictures. They could see from the condition of the snow that none of the attacking infantry had gone through the field where the bodies were located. Later that evening, the infantry battalion commander was contacted to ensure that the field would not be disturbed by his troops during the night.

The following morning, the field was still in an undisturbed condition. A platoon of engineers, two signal corps photographers, a group of graves registration personnel, a medical officer, and quartermaster service personnel began a systematic search of the field. The searchers initially used mine detectors as there had been considerable evidence that the Germans were booby-trapping the equipment of dead Americans in that vicinity. A mine detector located the first body and the searchers carefully removed the snow to take pictures. A photographer took pictures of each body and group of bodies as they became visible. During the three days of intensive searching, the men found seventy-one bodies. Three of the recovered bodies belonged to men killed before or after the massacre.* * *

---

* * * T/4 Cecil J. Cash and T/5 Raymond A. Heitman, C Battery, 197th Automatic Anti-Aircraft Weapons Battalion, were on their way by jeep to the 304th Ordnance Company in Malmédy. They left their company, located about eight miles east of Baugnez, just after lunch on December 17. They probably drove to Malmédy by N32 that runs through Waimes and Baugnez on its way to Malmédy. Their jeep must have passed Bagatelle, where the road from Thirimont joins N32, just before the Spitze opened fire on the 285th convoy. About 300 yards from the

Graves registration personnel tagged each body. The medical officer at the scene, Capt. John N. Snyder, examined most of the bodies and made notes as to their condition. All the bodies were frozen; approximately two feet of snow had covered them for nearly a month and the temperature had been below freezing for most of this period.

Lt. Col. Alvin B. Welsch, Inspector General's Office, was present and personally supervised the uncovering of the bodies. From his personal observation, he noted that most of the bodies had multiple wounds, apparently from small arms fire particularly in the temples, foreheads and the backs of the head. One of the bodies examined by Capt. Snyder had a bullet wound in the temple. The powder burns around the bullet indicated that this man had been shot at extremely close range.

The bodies were frozen to the ground and were twisted and stiff. The frozen state of the bodies made it very difficult to lift them onto the litters. The rescuers made no attempt to remove any articles of clothing or equipment from the bodies while in the field or while being transported to Malmédy. Nor did the men attempt any detailed examination of bullet or other wounds due to the frozen condition of the bodies. The enemy artillery shelling continued during the removal operation and precluded any thorough examination in the field.

---

crossroads at Baugnez, they were fired upon and crashed into the ditch on the north side of the road. As they crawled from the jeep, they found a Belgian boy, Peter Lentz, age fifteen, taking cover from the German fire. According to Lentz, "Three or four German vehicles came west on N32. One of the vehicles stopped and a young SS soldier jumped out of the vehicle and ordered them out of the ditch. Hardly had the three gotten out of the ditch when this young soldier shot both Cash and Heitman. Luckily, Peter Lentz spoke German. He told the young SS man that his brother was in the German Army, and he shouldn't shoot the brother of one of his comrades. The German then told him to leave. As Lentz was leaving, he heard the German fire several more shots into Cash and Heitman. At this point, a German officer came over to the young soldier and told him that was the way to fight in the old SS spirit."

On January 3, 1945, B Company, 526th Armored Infantry Battalion, was ordered to make an attack on the high ground a few thousand yards to the front of the area around the village of Hedomont. This attack moved B Company through the area west of Baugnez. The cost to B Company was high. Nineteen men were killed and eighteen were missing. Pvt. Delbert J. Johnson was one of the missing. According to Dick Stone, a member of B Company, he last saw Johnson disappearing into the early morning fog. The assumption is that Johnson was killed in the area of the massacre and discovered with the men that had escaped west on the road to Hedomont.

Body of Pfc. Klukavy as found in field, west of house #6. (Back of Café Bodarwe)

Massacre site, looking northeast. Crossroads in left center.

Looking southeast towards house #9.

Body of T/Sgt. Davidson,
as found in field.

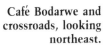

Massacre site. Café
Bodarwe in background.

Café Bodarwe and
crossroads, looking
northeast.
*Photos Courtesy of
National Archives*

*Photos on these two pages
were classified "Secret" at the
time they were taken.*

A few of the bodies showed torso lacerations, apparently caused by postmortem artillery shell fire. These men lay in the immediate vicinity of shell craters in the field. Several bodies had either one or both eyes removed, either by humans or animals, and the empty eye sockets were filled with snow. One body was stretched out on the ground, lying on its stomach, with the back of the head completely bashed in. At approximately 1:00 P.M. on January 14, 1945, the graves registration personnel began removing the bodies from the field, aided by personnel from the 3200 Quartermaster Service Company as litter bearers. The American personnel placed each body on a litter, carried the litters to a point several hundred yards down the road toward Malmédy, and loaded the litters on a 6 x 6 cargo truck which hauled them to Malmédy.

Late in the evening of January 14, the soldiers suspended operations due to darkness and extremely heavy enemy artillery concentrations. Most of the bodies had been removed from the field and taken into Malmédy. Early the following morning, rescuers removed the remaining bodies. At that time there was no evidence that any of the frozen bodies had been disturbed in any manner. The Americans found a few additional bodies under the snow in adjacent areas and removed them to Malmédy as well.

The bodies were delivered to a partially heated railroad control tower building in Malmédy. Here medical officers, graves registration personnel, and men from the Office of the Inspector General examined the bodies in detail. The medical personnel found the bodies still frozen and stiff even after several hours of being in the half-heated building and experienced considerable difficulty in removing the clothing and equipment from the bodies because of their frozen condition. It was difficult to unbutton pockets and the medical personnel found it necessary to use razor blades or sharp knives to cut the clothing and remove articles from pockets.

The Office of the Inspector General, Headquarters First Army, supervised the taking of photographs of the bodies when they came to the control tower in Malmédy. All photographs became part of the original investigation report and indicated the conditions of the bodies as they existed during the removal and examination. In the report, the medical officers described the dead soldiers' wounds, the property found on the bodies, and the condition of each body.

It was easy to identify the bodies because the weather had been below freezing for most of the time from December 17, 1944, to January 13, 1945, and two feet of snow had blanketed the area during the latter part of December. The extremely cold weather froze the bodies in the exact positions in which they were killed. Some of the dead still had their hands above their heads. Medical personnel performed autopsies on January 14-16, and the dead soldiers were interred in Henri Chapelle American Military Cemetery, Belgium, on January 17, 1945.

Not all of the bodies were located during this time due to the snow and their being scattered over a wide area. The men listed below were not located during this time but were found a day or two before their burial date. Most of these men were interred at Henri Chapelle Military Cemetery on the dates indicated.

Clark, Frederick	Pfc.	February 7, 1945
Davis, Warren	Pfc.	February 7, 1945
Goffman, Solomon S.	2nd Lt.	February 7, 1945
Jones, Wilson M., Jr.	T/5	April 1, 1945
Lester, Raymond E.	Cpl.	February 8, 1945
Lucas, Alan M.	T/4	February 7, 1945
Moore, William H.	Cpl.	April 14, 1945
Murray, David M.	Pfc.	February 24, 1945
Perkowski, Walter J.	Pvt.	February 7, 1945
Rupp, John M., Jr.	T/4	February 7, 1945
Stabulis, Alphonso J.	Sgt.	April 15, 1945
Thomas, Elwood E.	Pvt.	MIA
Vairo, Louis A.	Pvt.	February 8, 1945

Sgt. Alphonso Stabulis, T/5 Wilson Jones, Jr., and Cpl. William Moore were listed as unknown or missing in action until 1948-1949, when their bodies were disinterred and identified through pathological methods and dental records. These men were not recovered until April 1945, and had been buried in the Ardennes American Military Cemetery in Belgium.

Sgt. Stabulis was probably killed at the southern end of the area. Lt. Goffman was supposedly shot near Café Bodarwe for protesting the taking of personal items by members of Kampfgruppe

Pvt. Louis Vairo at Camp Gruber, Oklahoma, 1943.
Courtesy of Al Valenzi

Peiper. Pvt. John Cobbler died of his wounds in an aid station the day after the massacre. The nine other men — Pfc. Clark, Pfc. Davis, T/5 Jones, Cpl. Lester, T/4 Lucas, Cpl. Moore, Pfc. Murray, Pvt. Perkowski, and T/4 Rupp — were probably killed in action during the first part of the battle. Their bodies were scattered along the entire nine hundred yard area. Pvt. Louis A. Vairo was found eighteen kilometers east of Baugnez in Neuhof, Germany, and Pvt. Elwood E. Thomas was reported as missing in action.

According to information recently discovered in the National Archives, Pvt. Thomas was still alive, but seriously wounded, five days after the battle. This is the story from the statement of Mike Skoda.

I hid out in this barn. After five days they captured me again and took me to the same place (Baugnez Crossroads) and these paratroopers said "one of your comrades is lying out there." I said that I would like to see him. They took me to another barn and there was a fellow from my battery lying there very badly wounded. His back was so bad that he couldn't move. His name was Pvt. Thomas. I forget his first name.[90]

The statement of Henri Lejoly, age 50, of Baugnez tells what happened to either Pvt. Louis Vairo or Pvt. Thomas (first listed as missing in action, and later declared dead). His house was house #7 just northwest of the crossroads.

I heard several machine guns firing. I went downstairs to the door and saw some American soldiers running close to my house in a westerly and northwesterly direction. The American soldiers ran in several small groups. I stayed in the house the rest of the day and did not see anything more. The next day I found two wounded American soldiers in a shed by my house. There were also two dead American soldiers on the ground west

Quartermaster troops removed the bodies from the massacre field in January 1945 and placed them on trucks to be taken to Malmédy.

The body of Sgt. Donald Geisler as he was being taken into the building in Malmédy where the autopsies were performed.

Photos Courtesy of National Archives

In 1945, Cpl. Lawrence Martin was buried (top) in Henri Chapelle American Military Cemetery, Belgium. At the end of the war the families had the option of leaving the bodies overseas or returning them to the States. Cpl. Martin's body was returned to the States to his final resting place in High Street Cemetery, Rocky Mount, Virginia (bottom).

Photo above Courtesy of Donald Bower

Lt. Perry L. Reardon's Grave in Manning, South Carolina
Courtesy of Mrs. Julia Richburg (Reardon's widow)

Lt. Solomon Goffman's Grave in Emerson, New Jersey

of my house. My cousin, Henri Lejoly, came to my house and found the two wounded soldiers in the shed. He and my wife and daughter gave them first aid treatment, food, and drinks. We left them out in the shed because we were afraid of the Germans. Two German soldiers came and found these wounded Americans in the shed on Monday, December 18. One of the German soldiers wanted to kill them but the other one kept him from doing it. After one or two days, one of the American soldiers died, and we took him out of the shed and placed him on the ground. [This was probably Sgt. John Osborne.] German soldiers continued to come to the house for several days. They came in pairs and each time there would be a good one and a bad one. The bad one would always want to shoot the wounded Americans but the good one would always prevent it. On Wednesday, following the shooting at the cross roads, we received artillery fire from the American side and my family was taken by the Germans to a nearby house [House #8] where we stayed in the cellar until January 1, 1945, when it was set on fire. While we were at this house, some German soldiers said that the wounded American soldier in the shed at my house had been picked up and carried away.[91]

Including Thomas, Vairo and Cobbler, the Germans killed eighty-two men during the atrocity at Baugnez, Belgium, on December 17, 1944. This includes approximately sixty-six men from B Battery, three men from Headquarters Battery, 285th Field Artillery Observation Battalion, four men from Reconnaissance Company, 32nd Armored Regiment, 3rd Armored Division, two men from the 200th Field Artillery Battalion, two men from the 546th Ambulance Battalion, four from the 575th Ambulance Company, and one man from the 86th Engineer Battalion HP.

Of the survivors, forty-one were from B Battery; seven from Reconnaissance Company, 32nd Armored Regiment, 3rd Armored Division; one from C Company, 518th MP Battalion; one from M Company, 23rd Infantry Regiment, 2nd Infantry Division; and four from the 575th Ambulance Company. There were a total of fifty-four survivors including the five men who became prisoners of war and the five from the front of the convoy who escaped into the woods. Not included as a survivor was Cpl. David L. Lucas, who died as a POW on March 3, 1945.

At the time of the writing of this book, there are approximately twenty survivors still living.

ENDNOTES

A note on the translations. All translations are from official United States Army files. There are seven important quotations which are taken from the person spoken to or other witnesses of the statements. They are on pages 4, 14, 16, 20, 25, and 69. Each of them is in quotation marks, but is flagged by phrases indicating that these are paraphrases or quotations based on the memory of the witness. Secondly, the expression "bump them off" used in this book is the contemporary translator's words.

1. National Archives War Crimes Files, Malmédy, United States vs. Valentine Bersin, et al., Dachau, RG 153 & RG 338, Case 6-24, NARA Suitland Reference Branch, Suitland, Md.

2. *Ibid.*

3. *Ibid.*

4. *Ibid.*

5. *Ibid.*

6. *Ibid.*

7. *Ibid.*

8. *Ibid.*

9. *Ibid.*

10. Nobecourt, Jacques, *Hitler's Last Gamble.* Schocken Books, New York, 1967, p. 126. Translated from the French by R. H. Berry. Original source *Le Dernier Coup des de Hitler.* English copyright © Chatto & Windus, 1967, London SW1V 25A.

11. War Crimes 6-24.

12. *Ibid.*

13. *Ibid.*

14. *Ibid.*

15. Kane, *The 1st SS Panzer Division in the Battle of the Bulge,* World War II Historical Society, Bennington, Vermont, No. 2, (1988): p. 8.

16. Hechler, Kenneth W., *World War II German Military Studies,* Vol. 10, Interview with Oberst Joachim Peiper, Collection of 213 Special Reports, (Washington, D.C.: United States Army, 1949), p. 6.

17. *Ibid.*

18. *Ibid.*, p. 9.

19. *Ibid.*, p. 15.

20. *Ibid.*, p. 16.

21. *Ibid.*, p. 17.

22. *Ibid.*, p. 17.

23. *Ibid.*, War Crimes 6-24.

24. *Ibid.*, War Crimes 6-24.

25. Statement of Max Rieder, National Archives War Crimes Files, Malmédy, United States vs. Valentine Bersin, et al., Dachau, RG 153 & RG 338, Case 6-24, NARA Suitland Reference Branch, Suitland, Md.

26. National Archives War Crimes Files, Malmédy, United States vs. Valentine Bersin, et al., Dachau, RG 153 & RG 338, Case 6-24, NARA Suitland Reference Branch, Suitland, Md.

27. *Ibid.*

28. *Ibid.*

29. *Ibid.*

30. *Ibid.*

31. *Ibid.*

32. *Ibid.*

33. *Ibid.*

34. *Ibid.*

35. *Ibid.*

36. *Ibid.*

37. *Ibid.*

38. *Ibid.*

39. *Ibid.*

40. *Ibid.*

41. *Ibid.*

42. *Ibid.*

43. *Ibid.*

44. *Ibid.* This piece of paper still resides at the National Archives.

45. National Archives War Crimes Files, Malmédy, United States vs. Valentine Bersin, et al., Dachau, RG 153 & RG 338, Case 6-24, NARA Suitland Reference Branch, Suitland, Md.

46. *Ibid.*

47. Bacon, Thomas, "Malmédy Massacre," interview by John M. Bauserman, September 10, 1988.

48. Bechtel, Ernest, Letter to John M. Bauserman, 1989.

49. *Ibid.*, War Crimes 6-24.

50. MacDonald, Charles B., *A Time For Trumpets*, New York: William Morrow and Company, Inc., p. 215.

51. Pergrin, David, Conversation with author, August 1993.

52. Giles, Janice, *The Damned Engineers*, Boston: Houghton Mifflin Co., 1970, p. 156.

53. Bacon, Thomas, Letter to John M. Bauserman, 1988.

54. *Ibid.*, War Crimes 6-24.

55. *Ibid.*, War Crimes 6-24.

56. *Ibid.*, War Crimes 6-24.

57. *Ibid.*, War Crimes 6-24.

58. *op. cit.*, MacDonald, p. 217.

59. *Ibid.*, War Crimes 6-24.

60. *Ibid.*, War Crimes 6-24.

61. *Ibid.*, War Crimes 6-24.

62. Valenzi, Al, Conversation with author, August 1993.

63. *Ibid.*, War Crimes 6-24.

64. *Ibid.*, War Crimes 6-24.

65. *op. cit.*, MacDonald, p. 218.

66. *Ibid.*, War Crimes 6-24.

67. *Ibid.*, War Crimes 6-24.

68. *op. cit.*, Bacon letter, 1988.

69. *Ibid.*

70. After Action Report, 200th Field Artillery Battalion, RG 407, Entry 427, NARA Suitland Reference Branch, Suitland, Md.

71. Zach, Henry, Telephone conversation with John M. Bauserman, June 1988.

72. National Archives War Crimes Files, Malmédy, United States vs. Valentine Bersin, et al., Dachau, RG 153 & RG 338, Case 6-24, NARA Suitland Reference Branch, Suitland, Md.

73. Merriken, William, Letter to author, June 1988.

74. War Crimes 6-24, Suitland Reference Branch, National Archives, Suitland, Maryland, RG 153 & RG 338.

75. *Ibid.*

76. *Ibid.*

77. *Ibid.*

78. *Ibid.*

79. *Ibid.*

80. *Ibid.*

81. *Ibid.*

82. National Archives War Crimes Files, Malmédy, United States vs. Valentine Bersin, et al., Dachau, RG 153 & RG 338, Case 6-24, NARA Suitland Reference Branch, Suitland, Md.

83. Merriken, William, Letter to John M. Bauserman, June 1988.

84. *op. cit.*, War Crimes 6-24.

85. *Ibid.*

86. *Ibid.*

87. MacDonald, Charles B., *A Time For Trumpets*, William Morrow Company, 1985, p. 222.

88. Skoda, Mike, Newspaper Article, *Tribune Review*, Greensburg, Pa., 1983.

89. This was Fragmentary Order 27. "There is no evidence, however, that American troops took advantage of orders, implicit or explicit, to kill their SS prisoners." Cole, Hugh M., *The Ardennes: Battle of the Bulge*, Washington, D.C., U.S. Government Printing Office, 1965, p. 264.

90. National Archives War Crimes Files, Malmédy, United States vs. Valentine Bersin, et al., Dachau, RG 153 & RG 338, Case 6-24, NARA Suitland Reference Branch, Suitland, Md.

91. *Ibid.*

APPENDIX A

Autopsy Reports

All of Appendix A came from War Crimes 6-24, Modern Military Records Center, National Archives, Suitland, Maryland, Record Groups 153 & 338.

The bodies of the Americans were discovered in the field to the south of the crossroads. As the bodies were found, they were tagged with numbers. Body **#45** was Pvt. Paul Carr; body **#46** was T/5 James E. Luers; body **#47** was T/4 Thomas F. Watt.

Tag #3

"**Identified as: Luke S. Swartz, 33497309, T/5, Btry B, 285th FA Obsn. Bn.**

Personal effects found: One fountain pen, two pencils, one chain, one New Testament, one comb, letters, one pocket knife, one wallet containing 55 German marks, and one good luck charm.

Description and condition of outer clothing before being disrobed: Overcoat, field jacket, sweater, OD shirt and trousers, leggings, and overshoes. T/5 insignia on overcoat. Identification band on right wrist, blood on the right trouser leg in the region of the knee.

Medical diagnosis: The arms are raised above the head. Old blood on face. Bullet wound perforating right knee, with fracture compound comminuted of the right knee joint. Bullet wound, left side of head, penetrating the left forehead just above the eye, with the wound showing definite powder burns. (Opinion: Wound of head inflicted by a pistol bullet at close range.)"*

Tag #12

"Identified as: Robert (NMI) Cohen, 33477788, Pfc, Btry B, 285th FA Obsn. Bn.

Personal effects found: One comb, one flashlight, one pocket knife, one small chain, thirteen assorted coins, two cigarette lighters, one box needles, one tooth brush, one fountain pen, one pay book, one book in Hebrew, letters, wallet containing Belgian francs, 101 German marks.

Description and condition of outer clothing before being disrobed: Not taken on this body.

Medical diagnosis: Machine gun wounds, perforating, right upper chest with entrance posteriorly and exit anteriorly. GSW's perforating, head, entrance right forehead, exit posteriorly. Wound, entrance right temporal region, exit left temporal frontal region. Powder burns present at the entrance region of both wounds of the forehead. Wound, shrapnel, HE, right hand, traumatic amputation of whole hand at the wrist, post mortem. (Opinion: Wound of head inflicted by pistol bullet at close range.)"*

Tag #13

"Identified as: Gilbert R. Pittman, 3560418, Pvt, Btry B, 285th FA Obsn. Bn.

Personal effects found: Black wallet, pocket comb, dog tags, soldier's pay book, ring on the fourth finger left hand, photographs, leather photo folder.

Description and condition of outer clothing before being disrobed: Not taken on this body.

Medical diagnosis: Compound comminuted fracture of the skull with all of the skull missing including the base of the skull. Complete decerebration. Both eyes are missing: portion of the left nostril missing and all of the skin of the left cheek is missing. Scalp with its hair is still intact and is attached posteriorly only. Gun shot wound in the glands of the penis. Two gun shot wounds of left thigh; one about one inch above the knee joint and the other in the middle third of the thigh. Large gun shot wound of left leg with compound comminuted fracture of tibia and fibula."*

Tag #19

"Identified as: Elmer W. Wald, 20326296, Pfc, Med. Det., 200th FA Bn.

Personal effects found: Medical brassard, pen knife, fountain pen, comb, assorted coins, pencil, paybook, wallet containing one ten dollar bill, one two dollar bill, and 40 Belgian francs.

Description and condition of outer clothing before being disrobed: Mackinaw, field jacket, sweater, OD trousers and shirt, paratrooper's boots.

Medical diagnosis: Hands above head. Medical brassard securely attached to the left arm, definitely visible. High explosive missile wounds. Head: Lacerating wound of the head, involving occipital, parietal, and the frontal bones of the right side with complete loss of the brain tissue. Wound, perforating, left axilla caused by bullet. Wound, lacerating and perforating of the left hand caused by bullet. Opinion: The head wound appears to have been caused by a heavy missile; the wounds of the left axilla by bullets. Severe wound, lacerating, of the left hip, left upper thigh. This wound is caused by HE shell fire, and medical opinion is that it occurred after the soldier's death, no evidence of old blood being found."*

Tag #21

"Identified as: Halsey J. Miller, 32561864, Cpl., Btry B, 285th FA Obsn. Bn.

Personal effects found: Two rolls film, one chain, letters, prayer book, one fountain pen, soldier's pay book, wallet containing one dollar bill, 1 and ½ German marks, 5 French francs, 8 coins, one screwdriver.

Description and condition of outer clothing before being disrobed: OD shirt and trousers, leggings, shoes, overcoat, wool knit cap, gloves.

Medical diagnosis: Bullet wound penetrating left anterior chest wall slightly lateral to the midline and on the level of the nipple line. Wound, perforating, of head. Entrance posterior, in the region of the left parietal occipital bones. Exit, right forehead, slightly above and lateral to the eyebrow. Wound, lacerating, severe, of the right posterior surface of the knee, with fracture compound comminuted of the right knee joint. No powder burn could be found in the region of the entrance of the bullet in the head wound; however, it is the opinion of the medical officer that it was a close range shot, because the soldier was lying on his face at the time he was shot. The reason for soldier falling on his face was the wound described in the chest wall. The wound of the right knee is a post mortem wound, caused by high explosive shell fragments."*

APPENDIX B

Locations of the Remains

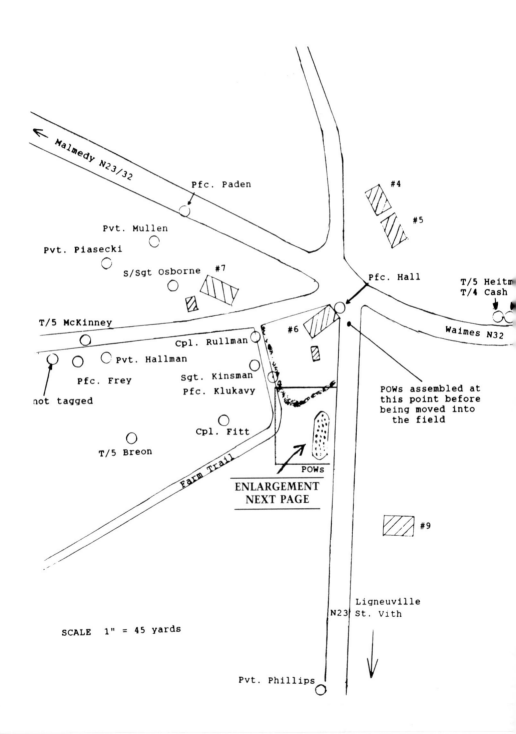

← Malmedy N23/32

Pfc. Paden

#4

#5

Pvt. Mullen

Pvt. Piasecki

S/Sgt Osborne   #7

Pfc. Hall

T/5 Heitm
T/4 Cash

Waimes N32

T/5 McKinney

Cpl. Rullman   #6

Pvt. Hallman

Pfc. Frey   Sgt. Kinsman
                 Pfc. Klukavy

not tagged

POWs assembled at
this point before
being moved into
the field

Cpl. Fitt

T/5 Breon

Farm Trail

POWs

ENLARGEMENT
NEXT PAGE

#9

Ligneuville
N23 St. Vith

SCALE   1" = 45 yards

Pvt. Phillips

ENLARGEMENT OF POW AREA

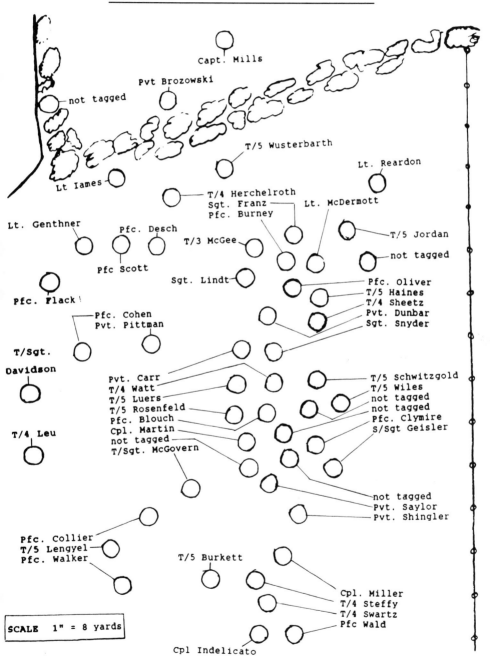

APPENDIX C

Causes of Death

Shot in the Head

Bloom, Donald L. Pvt.
Brozowski, Joseph A. Cpl.
Burkett, Samual P. T/5
Burney, L. M. Pfc.
Carson, Homer S. Pfc.
Cohen, Robert Pfc.
Collier, John D. T/5
Desch, Howard C. Pfc.
Dunbar, William J. Pvt.
Fitt, Carl B. Cpl.
Flack, Donald P. Pfc.
Frey, Carl B. Pfc.
Geisler, Donald E. S/Sgt.
Genthner, Carl R. 1/Lt.
Herchelroth, Sylvester V. Cpl.
Iames, Lloyd A. 2/Lt.
Indelicato, Ralph J. Cpl.
Lester, Raymond E. Cpl.
Leu, Selmer H. T/4
Lindt, Benjamin Sgt.
Luers, James E. T/5
Martin, Lawrence Cpl.
McDermott, Thomas E. 1/Lt.
Miller, Halsey, J. Cpl.
Mills, Roger J. Capt.
Mullen, Keston E. Pvt.
Munzinger, John S. 1/Lt.
Oliver, Thomas W. Pfc.

Paden, Paul L. Pfc.
Phillips, Peter R. Pvt.
Piasecki, Stanley F. Pvt.
Rullman, Carl H. Cpl.
Schwitzgold, Max T/5
Scott, Wayne L. Pvt.
Sheetz, Irwin M. T/4
Shingler, John H. Pvt.
Stevens, Carl M. Cpl.
Swartz, Luke S. T/5
Wald, Elmer W. Pfc.
Wusterbarth, Dayton E. T/5

Shrapnel

Davis, Warren Pfc.
Perkowski, Walter J. Pvt.
Rupp, John M. Jr. T/4

Died from Bleeding

Blough, Carl H. T/5
Carr, Paul R. Pvt.
Klukavy, John Pfc.
Walker, Richard B. Pfc.

Died from Blow to the Head

Breon, Charles R. T/5
Laufer, Howard W. T/5
Osborne, John D. S/Sgt.

High Explosive Shells

Clymire, John J. Pfc.
Haines, Charles F. T/5
Rosenfeld, George R. T/5

Concussion

Clark, Frederick Pfc.

Machine Gun or Small Arms Fire

Coates, James H. Pvt.
Cobbler, John H. Pvt.
Franz, Walter A. Sgt.
Goffman, Solomon S. 2/Lt.
Hallman, Samuel A. Pvt.
Jones, Wilson M. Jr. T/5
Jordan, Oscar R. Cpl.
Lengyel, Alfred Jr. T/5
McGee, James G T/3
McGovern, William T. T/Sgt.
O'Grady, David T. Cpl.
Pittman, Gilbert R. Pvt.
Reardon, Perry L. 1/Lt.
Saylor, Oscar Pvt.
Snyder, Robert J. Sgt.
Stabulis, Alphonse J. Sgt.
Steffy, George B. T/4
Watt, Thomas F. T/5
Wiles, Vester H. T/5

Crushed

Lucas, Allen M. T/4
McKinney, Robert L. T/5
Moore, William H. Cpl.

Unknown

Davidson, Paul G. T/Sgt.
Hall, Charles E. Pfc.
Kinsman, Alfred Sgt.
Murray, David M. Pfc.

Officially Declared Dead

Thomas, Elwood E. Pvt.

APPENDIX D

Final Burial Sites

Killed in Action (Baugnez) Massacre 12-17-1944

Battery B 285th Field Artillery Observation Bn.

1. Bloom, Donald L. Pvt.
   Bellefonte Union Cemetery
   Bellefonte, Penna.

2. Blouch, Carl H. T/5
   12-2881
   Arlington National Cemetery
   Washington, D.C.

3. Breon, Charles R. T/5
   Lot 37, Section 7, Grave 2
   Centre County Memorial Park
   1032 Benner Pike
   State College, Penna.

4. Brozowski, Joseph A. Cpl.
   C-8-30
   Henri-Chapelle, Belgium

5. Burkett, Samuel P. T/5
   Dry Ridge Cemetery
   Buffalo Mills, Penna.

6. Carr, Paul R. T/5
   D-8-21
   Henri-Chapelle, Belgium

7. Carson, Homer S. Pfc.
   New Paris Upper Cemetery
   New Paris, Penna.

8. Clark, Frederick Pfc.
   Section II, Grave 370
   Gettysburg National
   Cemetery
   Gettysburg, Penna.

9. Coates, James H. Pvt.
   Kilmarnock Cemetery
   Kilmarnock, Va.

10. Cobbler, John H. Pvt.
    A-18-43
    Henri-Chapelle, Belgium

11. Cohen, Robert Pfc.
    12-3228
    Arlington National Cemetery
    Washington, D.C.

12. Collier, John D. T/5
    Located in a field
    South of Fredericksburg, Va.

13. Davis, Warren Pfc.
C-10-59
Henri-Chapelle, Belgium

14. Davidson, Paul G. T/Sgt.
Vets. Section
Section 38
Lot 300, Grave 181
Allegheny Cemetery
4734 Butler Street
Pittsburgh, Penna.

15. Desch, Howard C. Pfc.
St. Marks Cemetery
Susquehanna Street
Allentown, Penna.

16. Dunbar, William J. Pvt.
Cramer Lot
Lakeview Cemetery
Penn Yan, N.Y.

17. Fitt, Carl B. Cpl.
Lawnview Cemetery
Rockledge, Penna.

18. Flack, Donald P. Pfc.
Bellefonte Union Cemetery
Bellefonte, Penna.

19. Franz, Walter A. Sgt.
Lot A, Section 14
Ashland Cemetery
Ashland, Ky.

20. Frey, Carl B. Pfc.
Fairview Cemetery
Denver, Penna.

21. Geisler, Donald E. S/Sgt.
Bedford Co. Memorial Park
Bedford, Penna.

22. Goffman, Solomon S. 2nd Lt.
Block 19, Lot 10
Grave 3
Cedar Park Cemetery
Emerson, N.J.

23. Haines, Charles F. T/5
Drytown Cemetery
Drytown (Newtown), Penna.

24. Hallman, Samuel A. Pvt.
Prospect Hill Cemetery
Front Royal, Va.

25. Hall, Charles E. Pfc.
12-2851
Arlington National Cemetery
Washington, D.C.

26. Herchelroth, Sylvester T/4
Marietta Cemetery
Marietta, Penna.

27. Jones, Wilson M. Jr. T/4
A-32-39
Ardennes, Belgium

28. Jordan, Oscar T/4
Hyndman Cemetery
Hyndman, Penna.

29. Kinsman, Alfred W. Sgt.
D-7-41
Henri-Chapelle, Belgium

30. Laufer, Howard W. T/5
Lot 45, Grave 7
Mt. Hope Cemetery
1270 Frankstown Rd.
Penn Hills, Penna.

31. Lengyel, Alexander Jr. T/5
D-15-34
Henri-Chapelle, Belgium

32. Lester, Raymond E. Cpl.
    A-9-52
    Henri-Chapelle, Belgium

33. Leu, Selmer H. T/4
    Estabrooks Cemetery
    Fond du Lac, Wis.

34. Lucas, Alan M. T/4
    B-9-32
    Henri-Chapelle, Belgium

35. Luers, James E. T/5
    H-4-58
    Henri-Chapelle, Belgium

36. Martin, Lawrence Cpl.
    High St. Cemetery
    Rocky Mount, Va.

37. McKinney, Robert T/5
    Section 2-C, Grave 5258
    Richmond National
        Cemetery
    Richmond, Va.

38. Miller, Halsey J. Sgt.
    A-9-45
    Henri-Chapelle, Belgium

39. Moore, William H. Cpl.
    Section 12, Lot 25
    Row 2, Grave 45
    Homewood Cemetery
    Dallas & Aylesboro Ave.
    Pittsburgh, Penna.

40. Munzinger, John S. 1st Lt.
    H-8626
    Long Island Natl. Cemetery
    Long Island, N.Y.

41. Murray, David M. Pfc.
    Ostrander Lot
    Prospect Hill Cemetery
    Schuylerville, N.Y.

42. O'Grady, David T. Cpl.
    Section 16, Range 14
    Lot 42, Grave 2
    St. Joseph Cemetery
    Lynn, Mass.

43. Oliver, Thomas W. Pfc.
    Section F, Grave 534
    Ft. Harrison Natl. Cemetery
    Richmond, Va.

44. Osborne, John D. S/Sgt.
    Grave 358, S of Section B-1
    Ft. Snelling Natl. Cemetery
    7601 34th Avenue
    S. Minneapolis, Minn.

45. Perkowski, Walter J. Pvt.
    Section 60, Lot 47, Grave 1
    Calvary Cemetery
    Cleveland, Ohio

46. Phillips, Peter R. Pvt.
    St. Nicholas Cemetery
    Duquesne, Penna.

47. Piasecki, Stanley F. Pvt.
    A-9-41
    Henri-Chapelle, Belgium

48. Pittman, Gilbert R. Pvt.
    G-1-41
    Henri-Chapelle, Belgium

49. Reardon, Perry L. 1st Lt.
    Manning Cemetery
    Manning, S.C.

50. Rosenfeld, George R. T/5
    C-14-42
    Henri-Chapelle, Belgium

51. Rullman, Carl H. Cpl.
    Lot 60, Section 3, Grave 7
    Lakeside Cemetery
    Erie, Penna.

52. Rupp, John M. Jr. T/4
    Garden of Memory
    Lot 51, Grave 3
    Northumberland Memorial
       Park
    Rd. 4, Box 27
    Sunbury, Penna.

53. Saylor, Oscar Pvt.
    D-3886
    Camp Nelson National
    Cemetery
    Nicholasville, Ky.

54. Schwitzgold, Max T/5
    D-59
    Knesseth Israel Synagogue
    Gloversville, N.Y.

55. Sheetz, Irwin M. T/4
    Gravel Hill Cemetery
    Palmyra, Penna.

56. Shingler, John H. T/5
    Belleville Lutheran Cemetery
    Belleville, Penna.

57. Snyder, Robert J. Sgt.
    12-3595
    Arlington National Cemetery
    Washington, D.C.

58. Stabulis, Alphonse J. Sgt.
    C-21-19
    Ardennes, Belgium

59. Steffy, George H. T/4
    A-9-26
    Henri-Chapelle, Belgium

60. Stevens, Carl M. Pfc.
    C-13-19
    Henri-Chapelle, Belgium

61. Swartz, Luke S. T/5
    H-9-49
    Henri-Chapelle, Belgium

62. Thomas, Elwood E. Pvt.
    Wall of Missing
    Ardennes, Belgium

63. Vairo, Louis A. Pvt.
    12-2957
    Arlington National Cemetery
    Washington, D.C.

64. Walker, Richard B. Pfc.
    Morgan's Church Cemetery
    Moneta, Va.

65. Watt, Thomas F. T/4
    14 Soldiers Field
    Row 1, Space 5
    Linn Grove Cemetery
    Greeley, Colo.

66. Wiles, Vester H. T/5
    Mount View Cemetery
    Danville, Va.

**HQ Battery, 285th Field
Artillery Observation Bn.**

67. Indelicato, Ralph J. Cpl.
    Signorelli Plot
    Calvary Cemetery
    St. Louis, Mo.

68. Mills, Roger L. Capt.
    5-3005
    Ft. Gibson National Cemetery
    Ft. Gibson, Okla.

69. McGovern, William T. T/Sgt.
    Soldiers Plot R, Row 6,
       Grave 11
    Calvary Cemetery
    718 Hazelwood Ave.
    Pittsburgh, Penna.

200th Field Artillery Bn.

70. Lindt, Benjamin Sgt.
    Rocky Ford Cemetery
    Rocky Ford, Colo.

71. Wald, Elmer W. Pfc.
    Dalmatia Cemetery
    Dalmatia, Penna.

Recon Co. 32nd Arm'd. Regt.

72. Iames, Lloyd A. 2nd Lt.
    D-6-36
    Henri-Chapelle, Belgium

73. Klukavy, John Pfc.
    D-15-46
    Henri-Chapelle, Belgium

74. McDermott, Thomas E. Jr.
       1st Lt.
    Lot 23, Range 21
    Section 36, Grave 1
    Holy Cross Cemetery
    Yeadon, Penna.

75. McGee, James G. T/3
    D-11-56
    Henri-Chapelle, Belgium

76. Burney, L. M. Pfc.
    Oaklawn Cemetery/
       Woodlawn Cemetery
    Jonesboro, Ark.

77. Genthner, Carl R. 1/Lt.
    C-13-3
    Henri-Chapelle, Belgium

78. Paden, Paul Pfc.
    Old Washington Cemetery
    Old Washington, Ohio

79. Scott, Wayne L. Pvt.
    G-2-41
    Henri-Chapelle, Belgium

546th Ambulance Co.

80. Mullen, Keston E. Pvt.
    Akins Cemetery
    Akins, Okla. (Sallisaw)

81. Wusterbarth, Dayton E. T/5
    Woodlawn Cemetery
    Oconto Falls, Wis.

86th Engr. Bn. (Heavy Pontoon)

82. Clymire, John J. Pfc.
    D-11-58
    Henri-Chapelle, Belgium

APPENDIX E

Survivors

B BATTERY SURVIVORS
August 1993

Sitting L to R — * Kenneth Baumgartel, * Leon Scarbrough, George Fox, Tom Bacon, Ralph Logan, Harold Billow.

Standing L to R — Bill Merriken, Al Valenzi, Ted Paluch, * Bill Poorman, Eugene Garrett, * William Norfleet, Bobby Werth.

* *Not in massacre*

During their visit to Belgium in 1990, George Fox and Ted Flechsig sat on the bicycle they rode December 17, 1944, to escape the massacre site. With them is the Belgian, Clement Xhurdebise, who owned and kept the bicycle all these years.

SURVIVORS

B Battery 285th FAOB	Rank	Wounds	Date of Death
1— Ahrens, Kenneth F.	Sgt.	Back	
2— Appman, Charles F.	T/5		
3— Billow, Harold W.	T/5		
4— Butera, Mario	Pfc.	Foot	1988
5— Daub, Carl C.	T/5		
6— Day, Donald W.	Pvt.	Leg	
7— Flechsig, Theodore G.	T/5	Shoulder/Leg/Hand	1991
8— Fox, George L.	Cpl.		
9— Garstka, Paul	T/5		1977
10— Hardiman, Aubrey J.	Pfc.	Foot	1982
11— Horn, Harry C.	Pfc.	Arms/Stomach	

SURVIVORS *continued*

B Battery 285th FAOB	Rank	Wounds	Date of Death
12— Kailer, John R.	Pvt.	Chest/Arm	1988
13— Kingston, Kenneth E.	T/5	Leg	1984
14— Law, Ralph W.	Pfc.	Leg	1991
15— Lary, Virgil T.	1st Lt.	Leg/Foot	1981
16— Martin, Paul J.	Pfc.	Foot	1979
17— Mattera, James P.	Pvt.		
18— Merriken, William H.	S/Sgt.	Back	
19— Moucheron, Carl W.	T/5	Head	1972
20— O'Connell, John A.	T/5	Jaw/Shoulder	1985
21— Paluch, Ted J.	T/5		
22— Piscatelli, Peter C.	Pfc.	Arm	1993
23— Profanchick, Andrew J.	Pvt.		1966
24— Reem, William F.	Pvt.		
25— Sciranko, Michael T.	Cpl.	Leg	
26— Skoda, Michael J.	T/5	Shoulder	1989
27— Smith, Charles E.	Sgt.		1985
28— Smith, Robert L.	Pvt.		1989
29— Summers, William B.	T/5		
30— Valenzi, Albert M.	T/5	Legs	
31— Werth, Bobby	Pvt.	Legs	

575th Ambulance Co.			
32— Anderson, Roy B.	Pvt.	Foot	1983
33— Dobyns, Samuel	Pvt.	Arm/Ankle	1983
34— Domitrovich, Stephen J.	Pfc.		
35— McKinney, James M.	Pfc.		1978

Recon Co. 32nd Arm'd. Reg't., 3rd Arm'd. Div.			
36— Bojarski, Edward	Cpl.		1980
37— Lewis, Marvin J.	Sgt.	Leg	1979
38— Wendt, Walter J.	Cpl.	Arm	
39— Zach, Henry R.	S/Sgt.	Leg/Hip	

SURVIVORS *continued*

Co. M, 23rd Inf. Reg't., 2nd Inf. Div.	Rank	Wounds	Date of Death
40— Johnson, Herman	S/Sgt.		1984
Co. C, 518th MP Bn.			
41— Ford, Homer D.	Pfc.	Arm	1950

Men who drove vehicles away and became POWs.
B Battery, 285th FAOB

1— Bacon, Thomas J.	T/5		
2— Lacy, Eugene	Sgt.		
3— Logan, Ralph	T/5		
4— Lucas, D.L.	T/5		1945

Recon Co., 32nd Armored Reg't., 3rd Armored Div.

5— Anderson, Vernon	Sgt.		1985
6— Barron, William E.	Pvt.		
7— Cummings, J. I.	Cpl.		

Men who were not in the massacre field.
B Battery, 285th FAOB

1— Bower, Donald L.	Pfc.		1990
2— Conrad, Robert B.	Cpl.		1978
3— Garrett, Eugene H.	T/5		
4— Greaff, George E.	Cpl.		
5— Mearig, Robert P.	T/4		
6— Reding, Charles E.	T/5		
7— Schmitt, Warren R.	T/5		

SURVIVORS

Kenneth F. Ahrens worked for General Electric until his retirement. He lives in Kentucky with his wife Dottie and has six children and nine grandchildren.

Charles F. Appman worked as a surveyor and maintenance mechanic. He has three children. He is retired and spends his time reading and making models of WW II planes and vehicles. He resides in Pennsylvania.

Thomas J. Bacon was released from Stalag 11B in April 1945 by British forces and spent the next several months in hospitals. He graduated from Cornell University and retired from the Connecticut Department of Transportation in 1983. Tom and his wife (Ann) live in Connecticut.

Harold F. Billow worked for an AMP plant in Pennsylvania before his retirement. While recuperating from the massacre in England, he met an English girl (Vera). They were married exactly one year to the day after the massacre. They live in Pennsylvania and have two children and two grandchildren.

Donald L. Bower graduated from Ohio University with an M.A. and retired from teaching in Ohio. He married (Myrtle) and they had three children and six grandchildren. He died on October 11, 1990.

Mario "Boots" Butera worked for the city of New Kensington, Pennsylvania before his death in 1988. He was married and had two daughters.

Robert Conrad worked in Indiana until his death in 1978.

Carl C. Daub worked with Kenneth Kingston in the contracting business until 1973. He continued in this business till 1987 when he became mentally ill. He killed his wife in 1988 and has never been found. He has four sons.

Donald Day lives in New York and is a retired electrician. He and his wife (Jo) have three daughters and eight grandchildren.

Ted G. Flechsig received his B.A. from Rutgers University in 1950 and his M.A. from Johns Hopkins in 1953. He worked for the Federal Reserve Board until his retirement in the late 1980's. He married (Mary Lou) and had two sons. He died April 12, 1991.

George Fox worked for Avtex Fibers in Virginia before retiring in 1985. He met wife (Marge) on a blind date and they have two daughters and two grandchildren. They have been from Alaska to Florida, traveling in their Airstream trailer. He was reunited with Ted Flechsig with whom he had escaped, at a 285th reunion in 1988. They returned to Baugnez in 1990 and met the Belgian brothers who helped them escape.

Eugene Garrett married (Jackie) right after the war. They have three daughters and seven grandchildren. Gene worked in the petroleum industry until his retirement. The Garretts live in Oklahoma and enjoy boating.

Paul J. Garstka lived in Pennsylvania and died in 1977.

George E. Graeff's last known address was in Pennsylvania.

Aubrey J. Hardiman managed a Hunt Club in Virginia. He died in 1982.

Harry C. Horn is retired and enjoys hunting in Pennsylvania.

John R. Kailer graduated from Ohio State University and worked in the aerospace industry in California. He died on Memorial Day in 1988.

Kenneth E. Kingston worked in the produce business before entering the contracting business. He worked in this field until his death in 1984. He married (Virginia) and had a son and a daughter, and five grandchildren.

Eugene Lacy retired from government service and lives in Oklahoma.

Virgil T. Lary became an accountant before his death in 1981.

Ralph W. Law worked for an upholstery company in Virginia until his death in 1990.

Ralph Logan was released from Camp Zittau, a German work camp in Czechoslovakia. From there he hitched a ride to Frankfurt and was then returned to the States. He worked as an insurance agent for many years. He and his wife (Lorraine) have two boys and six grandchildren. He lives in Wisconsin.

P. J. Martin made his living as a farmer in North Carolina until his death in 1979.

James P. Mattera worked for the Pennsylvania Department of Highways. He resides in Pennsylvania.

Robert "Sketch" Mearig retired from the U.S. Postal Service after thirty years of service. He married (Betty) and has two children and five grandchildren. He likes to refinish antiques and is a town historian in Pennsylvania.

William H. "Bill" Merriken returned from the service and finished college. He opened a Plumbing, Heating and Air-conditioning business in 1947 which he operated till 1969. After that he worked for the state of Virginia as a Senior Auditor. He retired in 1985. He married (Betty) and has four daughters and five grandchildren. He likes woodworking and reading. He finally located "Chuck" Reding who had helped him escape. In 1989 they met on Memorial Day weekend for the first time since 1944.

Carl W. Moucheron died in 1972. He lived in Pennsylvania.

John A. O'Connell worked for the ITT Corporation before becoming a real estate broker in 1972. He was married and had eight children. He lived in Kansas and passed away in 1985.

Ted Paluch is a retired traffic manager and lives in New Jersey.

Peter C. Piscatelli lived in New York before his death in February 1993.

Andrew S. Profanchick lived in Ohio before he died in 1966.

Charles E. Reding is retired and lives in Louisiana. In 1989 Bill Merriken located him and they met later that year for the first time since they had parted three days after the atrocity. Neither had known what happened to the other those past forty-five years.

William P. Reem retired from Mars Candy Company in 1985 and lives in Pennsylvania. He is married and has five children, ten grandchildren and one great-grandchild.

Warren Schmitt is a retired Kansas real estate developer. He married (Phyllis) in 1946 and has four children and eight grandchildren.

Mike Sciranko worked in the automobile industry before retiring. He lives in Pennsylvania.

Michael J. Skoda married (Helen) and had two children and four grandchildren. He retired from U.S. Steel in the 80's and moved to Florida. He liked to golf and work around the house until his death in 1989.

Charles E. Smith lived in Pennsylvania. He died in 1985.

Robert L. Smith lived in Pennsylvania until his death in March 1989.

William B. "Bruce" Summers lives in West Virginia. He is married (Annetta) and they have three children, four grandchildren and four great-grandchildren. He retired from Dow Chemical Company as a regional manager.

Al Valenzi retired in 1984 after twenty-five years with the U.S. Postal Service. He is married (Virginia) and has one son, two grandchildren, and recently became a great-grandfather. He enjoys doing art work, reading and walking. He lives in Pennsylvania.

Bobby Werth lives in Texas with his wife (Genoa). He is retired from Texaco where he worked for thirty-six years. He enjoys hunting and fishing along with his six children, eleven grandchildren and eleven great-grandchildren.

Recon Co., 32nd Armored Reg't., 3rd Armored Div.

Vernon Anderson lived in Pennsylvania until his death in 1985.

William E. Barron lives in Tennessee and is still active in the cotton industry. He married (Dorothy), has three children and enjoys golfing and fishing.

Edward J. Bojarski worked in a paper mill in Wisconsin. He died in 1980.

J. I. Cummings is a retired excavation contractor and lives in California with his wife. He likes to travel and visit Las Vegas. He has four grown children.

Marvin J. Lewis died in May 1979.

Walter Wendt is eighty-two years old and enjoys retirement. He lives in Wisconsin, is married and has two sons and two grandchildren.

Henry R. Zach had to give up farming due to the wounds received at Baugnez (Malmédy). He retired from the U.S. Postal Service after thirty-three years. He is married and has one daughter. He lives in Wisconsin.

518th MP Co.

Homer D. Ford died in February 1950.

Co. M, 23rd Inf. Reg't., 2nd Inf. Div.

Herman Johnson retired from Mobile Oil. He was married and had one daughter. He died in 1975.

575th Ambulance Co.

Roy B. Anderson worked in the food processing business till his death in 1983.

Samuel Dobyns worked for the Ohio Department of Highways until he retired in 1976. He died in 1978.

Stephen Domitrovich is a retired businessman and lives with his wife (Dorothy) in Pennsylvania. He has two children and two grandchildren.

James M. McKinney lived in Indiana and passed away in 1978.

APPENDIX F

Killed In Action

December 17, 1944
Baugnez, Belgium

Bloom, Donald L. Pvt. . . . . Pennsylvania
Burney, L. M. Pvt. . . . . Arkansas
Blouch, Carl H. T/5 . . . . Pennsylvania
Breon, Charles R. T/5 . . . . Pennsylvania
Burkett, Samuel P. T/5 . . . . Pennsylvania
Carr, Paul R. T/5 . . . . West Virginia
Carson, Homer S. Pfc. . . . . Pennsylvania
Clymire, John J. Pfc. . . . . Michigan
Cobbler, John H. Pvt. . . . . Virginia
Collier, John D. T/5 . . . . Virginia
Cohen, Robert Pfc. . . . . Pennsylvania
Coates, James H. Pvt. . . . . Virginia
Davidson, Paul G. T/Sgt. . . . . Pennsylvania
Desch, Howard C. Pfc. . . . . Pennsylvania
Dunbar, William J. Pvt. . . . . Ohio
Fitt, Carl B. Cpl. . . . . Pennsylvania
Flack, Donald J. Pfc. . . . . Pennsylvania
Franz, Walter A. Sgt. . . . . Kentucky
Frey, Carl B. Pfc. . . . . Pennsylvania
Geisler, Donald E. S/Sgt. . . . . Pennsylvania
Genthner, Carl R. 1st Lt. . . . . New York
Haines, Charles F. T/5 . . . . Pennsylvania
Hall, Charles E. . . . . Washington, D.C.
Hallman, Samuel A. Pvt. . . . . Virginia
Herchelroth, Sylvester V. . . . . Pennsylvania
Iames, Lloyd A. 2nd Lt. . . . . California
Indelicato, Ralph J. Cpl. . . . . Missouri

Jordan, Oscar R. T/4 .... Pennsylvania
Kinsman, Alfred W. Sgt. .... Massachusetts
Klukavy, John Pfc. .... Michigan
Laufer, Howard W. T/5 .... Pennsylvania
Lengyel, Alexander, Jr. T/5 .... Ohio
Leu, Selmer H. T/4 .... Wisconsin
Lindt, Benjamin Sgt. .... Colorado
Luers, James E. T/5 .... Pennsylvania
Martin, Lawrence Cpl. .... Virginia
McDermott, Thomas E. 1st Lt. ...... Pennsylvania
McGee, James G. T/3 .... Pennsylvania
McGovern, William T. T/Sgt. .... Pennsylvania
McKinney, Robert L. T/5 .... Virginia
Miller, Halsey J. Sgt. .... New Jersey
Munzinger, John S. 1st Lt. .... New York
O'Grady, David T. Cpl. .... Massachusetts
Oliver, Thomas W. Pfc. .... Virginia
Osborne, John D. S/Sgt. .... Minnesota
Paden, Paul L. Pfc. .... Ohio
Phillips, Peter R. Pvt. .... Pennsylvania
Piasecki, Stanley F. Pvt. .... Illinois
Pittman, Gilbert R. Pvt. .... West Virginia
Reardon, Perry L. 2nd Lt. .... South Carolina
Rosenfeld, George R. T/5 .... New York
Rullman, Carl H. Cpl. .... Pennsylvania
Saylor, Oscar Pvt. .... Kentucky
Schwitzgold, Max T/5 .... New York
Scott, Wayne L. Pvt. .... Indiana
Sheetz, Irvin M. T/4 .... Pennsylvania
Shingler, John H. T/5 .... Pennsylvania
Snyder, Robert J. Sgt. .... Pennsylvania
Steffy, George H. 2 T/4 .... Pennsylvania
Stevens, Carl M. Pfc. .... Massachusetts
Swartz, Luke S. T/5 .... Pennsylvania
Vairo, Louis A. Pvt. .... Virginia
Wald, Elmer W. Pfc. .... Pennsylvania
Walker, Richard B. Pfc. .... Virginia
Watt, Thomas F. T/4 .... Colorado
Wiles, Vester H. T/5 .... Virginia
Wusterbarth, Dayton E. T/5 .... Wisconsin

APPENDIX G

German Table of Organization & Equipment

3rd PANZER PIONIER COMPANY (Armored Engineers)

Headquarters SPW

Obersturmführer	SIEVERS, FRANZ	Company Commander
Oberscharführer	SCHÄFER, WILLI	group leader
Rottenführer	GOTTSCHLICK,	driver
Rottenführer	SCHWALD,	messenger
Rottenführer	SCHLIEPMANN,	messenger
Unterscharführer	ROSE, HEINZ	medic
Rottenführer	BOBENBURGER,	
Sturmmann	EBERDING,	
Unterscharführer	BAER, PAUL	driver

1st Platoon

1-SPW

Unterscharführer	SEITZ, AUGUST	Platoon leader
Unterscharführer	BEIER, FRANZ	driver
Sturmmann	JANSEN, HEINRICKS	messenger

1st Squad

1-SPW

Rottenführer	TAUT, GERHARD	group leader
Rottenführer	SCHIRADO, HANS	driver
Sturmmann	GROBER,	driver

2-SPW
_____

Unterscharführer	DIXTRA, ALFRED	squad leader
Rottenführer	BAIER, FRANZ	driver
Sturmmann	TRATT, OSKAR	

2nd Squad

1-SPW
_____

Rottenführer	SCHOTT, HEINZ	group leader
Rottenführer	EICHLER, HEINZ	driver

2-SPW
_____

Rottenführer	VERSICK, HERBERT	squad leader
Sturmmann	ELSMANN, RUDI	driver

3rd Squad

1-SPW
_____

Rottenführer	STABE,	driver
Unterscharführer	STURZENBECKER,	group leader

2-SPW
_____

Rottenführer	MEINCKE,	driver

2nd Platoon

Platoon Leader's SPW
_____

Unterscharführer	BEUTNER, MAX	platoon leader
Rottenführer	GOLDSCHMIDT, ERNST	driver
Unterscharführer	DICKMANN, EDGAR	ass't squad leader
Rottenführer	DEIBERT, GEORGE	driver
Rottenführer	HAMMERER, MAX	messenger
Sturmmann	SCHLINGMANN, GERHARDT	messenger
Pionier	HANKE, WILLI	machine gunner

1st Squad

1-SPW

Unterscharführer	BODE, FRIEDEL	group leader
Rottenführer	MEIRER,	driver
Sturmmann	AISTLEITNER, JOHAN	machine gunner
Pionier	JIRASSEK, WERNER	machine gunner
Sturmmann	KIES, FRIEDEL	machine gunner
Sturmmann	SCHAEFFLER, ERNST	driver
Sturmmann	LOSENSKI, HERBERT	driver
Pionier	WASSENBERGER, JOHANN	machine gunner
Sturmmann	SCHULTE, BERTEL	driver

2nd Squad

1-SPW

Unterscharführer	WITKOWSKI, SEPP	group leader
Rottenführer	GEILHOFER,	driver
Pionier	TOEDTER, HANS	machine gunner
Pionier	STICKEL, HEINZ	machine gunner
Pionier	JÄKEL, SIEGFRIED	rifleman
Pionier	ENDE, HARRY	
Pionier	WALKOWIAK, GERHARD	
Pionier	HERGETH, EMIL	
Pionier	STORCH, HUBERT	
Sturmmann	HOFMANN, JOACHIM	driver
Sturmmann	NEVE, GUSTAV	driver

3rd Squad

1-SPW

Unterscharführer	ALTKRUGER, WOLFGANG	group leader
Sturmmann	SPRENGER, GUSTAV	driver
Sturmmann	BOLTZ, MARCEL	machine gunner
Sturmmann	KISSEWITZ, FRANZ	machine gunner
Sturmmann	MANS, GÜNTHER	driver
Sturmmann	MÜLLER, MANFRED	machine gunner
Rottenführer	GERHARZ, ALFRED	machine gunner

2-SPW

Rottenführer	OETTINGER, HANS	driver
Rottenführer	BILOCHETZKI, WILLI	group leader
Unterscharführer	MARTENS, HANNES	motor sgt.
Rottenführer	SCHNEIDER, HANS	machine gunner

9th PANZER PIONIER COMPANY (Armored Engineers)

Headquarters Company SPW

Obersturmführer	RUMPF, ERICH	company commander
Unterscharführer	HEGESTET, KARL HEINZ	radio operator
Rottenführer	WECK, RICHARD	orderly
Unterscharführer	KORFE, WALTER	clerk
Rottenführer	VIEL, KARL	driver
Rottenführer	HEIRENS, HEINZ	driver
Unterscharführer	MAUTE, ERICH	medic
Sturmmann	FRANKE,	

1st Platoon

Unterscharführer	HERING, GÜNTHER	platoon leader
Rank unk	BUTH, PAUL	driver
Sturmmann	PUPKULIES, FRITZ	machine gunner
Rank unk	SPAEH,	

1st Squad (2 SPW'S)

1-SPW

Rottenführer	WEMMEL, KARL	squad leader
Rank unk	HOEPPNER,	driver
Rank unk	ZIMMERMAN,	
Rank unk	RADANKE,	
Unterscharführer	HELD,	group leader
Sturmmann	FRANSEE, WALTER	radio operator

2-SPW

Rottenführer	OLROGGE, KARL	squad leader
Sturmmann	BUTTNER, HERMAN	driver
Sturmmann	SCHMIPEL, FERDINAND	driver
Sturmmann	LUSSEN, MANFRED	medic
Sturmmann	KAPPERMAN, HEINZ	radio operator
Rank unk	GRAMLICH,	rifleman
Rank unk	STECKNER,	rifleman
Rank unk	STEIGER,	machine gunner

2nd Squad

Unterscharführer	BRAUNROTH, JOACHIM	squad leader
Unterscharführer	RUMMEL,	motor sgt.
Unterscharführer	KORF, WALTER	maintenance chief
Schütze	TILL, FRED	machine gunner
Rank unk	QUOLKE, RUDI	
Rottenführer	PROBST, WILHELM	driver
Rank unk	BORCHERS, GÜNTER	

2nd Platoon

Rank unk	LENK,	platoon leader
Pionier	TOEDTER, HANS	driver
Pionier	STORCH, HUBERT	
Sturmmann	SUSSE,	

3rd Platoon

Unterscharführer	KUHN, WERNER	platoon leader

Penal/Disciplinary Platoon

Oberscharführer	WENDELEIT,	platoon leader

1st Squad

Unterscharführer	HASS, HELMUTH	squad leader
Unterscharführer	BIOTTA,	
Sturmmann	RIEDER, MAX	rifleman
Schütze	CORZIENI,	rifleman
Unterscharführer	VON CHAMIER, WILLI	machine gunner
Rottenführer	KATSCHER,	machine gunner
Sturmmann	BARTH, ARTHUR	
Unterscharführer	MODES,	

2nd Squad

Unterscharführer	PERSIN,	squad leader
Rottenführer	SCHMITT,	
Rank unk	RUGRIEGEL,	
Rank unk	BALNAT,	
Rank unk	SOMMER,	
Rank unk	DIETZ, REINHARDT	

PANZER #701

Hauptsturmführer	KLINGHOFER, OSCAR	Commander of 7th company
Sturmmann	REUSCH, HELMUT	radio operator
Sturmmann	MUHLBACH,	loader
Rottenführer	EHRHARDT, ROLF	driver

PANZER #702

Unterscharführer	SCHRADER, HEINZ	Panzer commander

PANZER #711

Untersturmführer	REHAGEL, HEINZ	Panzer commander
Sturmmann	BRANDT, WILLY	gunner
Sturmmann	FECHNER,	driver
Sturmmann	KUNZEL,	radio operator
Sturmmann	PIPER, JOACHIM	loader

PANZER #712

Oberscharführer	KOCH, WERNER	Panzer commander
Sturmmann	AHRENDS, EDWARDS	radio operator
Sturmmann	REICKE, WERNER	loader
Sturmmann	PARTENHEIMER, HEINZ	gunner
Rottenführer	OELGOETZ, JOSEP	driver

PANZER #713

Unterscharführer	DUBBERT, ERICH	Panzer commander
Sturmmann	STEPHAN, ANTON	radio operator
Rank unk	MULING,	gunner

PANZER #714

Unterscharführer	BURK, HENRICH	Panzer commander

PANZER #723

Oberscharführer	CLOTTEN, ROMAN	Panzer commander
Sturmmann	BOCK, HERMAN	gunner
Sturmmann	KAMMLER,	radio operator
Rottenführer	KOEBITZ, ERNST	driver
Schütze	GEHL,	loader

PANZER #731

Hauptscharführer	SIPTROTT, HANS	Panzer commander
Rottenführer	WENTENGEL,	gunner
Rottenführer	SCHAFFER, GERHARD	driver
Sturmmann	FLEPS, GEORG	loader
Sturmmann	ARNOLD,	radio operator

PANZER #734

Rank unk	PILARZEK,	Panzer commander
Rank unk	THORN, MANFRED	driver

LEAD PANZER IN SPITZE, PANZER #612/614

Obersturmführer	STERNEBECK, WERNER	Panzer commander
Rottenführer	ETZINGER, JOHANN	driver

PANZER #625

Oberscharführer	HUBER, HUBERT	Panzer commander
Sturmmann	GRIKSCHAS, MARTIN	gunner
Oberschütze	RAUCH, JOSEP	radioman
Schütze	SCHREIRER,	driver
Sturmmann	SCHRODER,	loader

PANZER #631

Rank unk	VIEN,	Panzer commander
Sturmmann	RAUEN, PETER	radio operator

PANZER #632

Oberscharführer	KUGEL,	Panzer commander
Rottenführer	KLEIN, PAUL	loader
Rank unk	NOACK,	radioman
Unterscharführer	KNORN,	driver
Sturmmann	HEINZ, DANIEL	gunner

PANZER #633

Unterscharführer	GAST,	Panzer commander
Rank unk	KETTE,	radio operator
Rank unk	MALIC,	gunner

PANZER #102

Hauptscharführer	SKOTZ,	Panzer commander
Rank unk	PEDERSEN,	driver
Rank unk	ZACKEL,	loader

PANZER #114

Unterscharführer	BRIESEMEISTER, KURT	Panzer commander
Rottenführer	HESS, JOSEPH	radio operator
Unterscharführer	NUECHTER,	loader
Unterscharführer	STORM, RUDI	driver
Rottenführer	TIELECHE, HANS	gunner

PANZER #221

Rank unk	KNAPPICH,	Panzer commander
Sturmmann	MIKOLASCHEK, ARNOLD	radio operator
Rottenführer	WERNER, ERICH	driver
Rottenführer	HOFFMAN, HEINZ	gunner

PANZER #225

Rank unk	BAIER, KURT	Panzer commander

APPENDIX H

Burial Sites of German Officers

Peiper's grave in Schöndorf am Ammersee, Germany.

Grave of Major Werner Poetschke, the officer who supposedly gave the order to fire. German Military Cemetery in Mattersburg, Austria.

SOURCES CONSULTED

BOOKS:

Cole, Hugh M. *The Ardennes: Battle of the Bulge.* Washington, D.C.: U.S. Government Printing Office, 1965.

Eisenhower, John S. D. *The Bitter Woods.* New York: G.P. Putnam, 1969.

Fowle, Barry W. and Floyd D. Wright. *The 51st Again! An Engineer Combat Battalion in World War II.* Shippensburg, Penna.: White Mane Publishing Co., Inc., 1992.

Giles, Janice Holt. *The Damned Engineers.* Boston: Houghton Mifflin Co., 1970.

Kane, Steven P. *1st SS Panzer Division in the Battle of the Bulge.* Bennington, Vt.: World War II Historical Society, 1988.

MacDonald, Charles B. *A Time for Trumpets.* New York: William Morrow and Co., 1970.

Merriam, Robert E. *Dark December.* New York: Ziff-Davis, 1947.

Nobecourt, Jacques. *Hitler's Last Gamble.* New York: Schocken Books, 1967. Translated from the French by R. H. Berry. Original source *Le Dernier Coup Des De Hitler.* English copyright: Chatto & Windus, London.

Pallud, Jean Paul. *Battle of the Bulge, Then and Now.* London: Battle of Britain Prints International Limited, 1984.

Pergrin, David. *First Across The Rhine.* New York: MacMillan Publishing Co., 1989.

Toland, John. *Battle.* New York: Random House, 1959.

Weingartner, James J. *Crossroads of Death.* Berkeley: University of California Press, 1979.

Whiting, Charles. *Massacre at Malmédy.* New York: Stein and Day, 1971.

OFFICIAL GOVERNMENT SOURCES:

After Action Reports, Unit Histories, RG 407, Entry 427, NARA Suitland Reference Branch, Suitland, Md.
  32nd Armored Infantry Regiment, Third Armored Division
  86th Engineer Battalion (Heavy Pontoon)
  120th Infantry Regiment, 30th Infantry Division
  190th Field Artillery Battalion
  197th Automatic Anti-Aircraft Weapons Battalion
  200th Field Artillery Battalion
  285th Field Artillery Observation Battalion
  291st Combat Engineer Battalion
  518th Military Police Battalion
  526th Armored Infantry Battalion
  546th Ambulance Company
  575th Ambulance Company
  3200th Quartermaster Service Company

National Archives War Crimes Files. Malmédy, United States vs. Valentine Bersin, et al., Dachau, RG 153, Case 6-24, Boxes 69-73.

National Archives War Crimes Files. Malmédy, United States vs. Valentine Bersin, et al., Dachau, RG 338, Case 6-24, Boxes 1-70. *Both record groups must be consulted by the researcher interested in the Malmédy Massacre.*

European Theater Interrogations (ETHINT) Series #10, OBERST (W-SS) Joachim Peiper, First SS Panzer Regiment. December 11-24, 1944, National Archives, Washington, D.C.

European Theater Interrogations (ETHINT) Series #11, OBERST (W-SS) Joachim Peiper, First SS Panzer Regiment. December 16-19, 1944, National Archives, Washington, D.C.

MANUSCRIPTS:

C Series. C-004, OBERST (W-SS) Joachim Peiper. "Kampfgruppe Peiper". December 15-26, 1944, National Archives, Washington, D.C.

Reynolds, M. F. Major General. *Exercise Pied Peiper.* Copy in possession of author.

Thompson, Royce L. The E.T.O. Ardennes Campaign, *Operations of the Combat Group Peiper.* December 16-26 1944. U.S. Army Center of Military History.

PERSONAL INTERVIEWS:

Ahrens, Ken.   13 September 1987. Pittsburgh, Penna.; 285th Reunion.

Bacon, Thomas.   10 September 1988. Lancaster, Penna.; 285th Reunion.

Barron, William.   5 November 1987. Memphis, Tenn.; Telephone.

Billow, Harold.   10 September 1988. Lancaster, Penna.; 285th Reunion.

Bower, Donald.   20 July 1987. Mt. Vernon, Ohio.

Daub, Carl.   15 December 1987. Whitehall, Penna.; Telephone.

Day, Donald.   2 February 1988. Balmat, N.Y.; Telephone.

Domitrovich, Stephen.   15 December 1988. Aliquippa, Penna.; Telephone.

Garrett, Eugene.   13 September 1987. Pittsburgh, Penna.; 285th Reunion.

Horn, Harry.   1 December 1987. Mann's Choice, Penna.; Telephone.

Kailer, John.   20 January 1988. Pomona, Calif.; Telephone.

Lacy, Eugene.   13 March 1988. Lawton, Okla.; Telephone.

Law, Ralph.   15 January 1988. Eden, N.C.; Telephone.

Logan, Ralph.   13 September 1987. Pittsburgh, Penna.; 285th Reunion.

Mattera, Jim.   13 April 1987. Media, Penna.

Mearig, Robert.   13 September 1987. Pittsburgh, Penna.; 285th Reunion.

Merriken, William.   12 May 1987. Charlottesville, Va.

Paluch, Ted.   11 September 1989. Morgantown, Penna.; 285th Reunion.

Pergrin, Dave.   13 April 1987, Media, Penna.; 11 September 1989, Morgantown, Penna.; 21 August 1993, Roanoke, Va.

Piscatelli, Peter.   10 September 1988. Lancaster, Penna.; 285th Reunion.

Reding, Charles.   28 January 1988. Houma, La.; Telephone.

Reem, William.   6 February 1989. Elizabethtown, Penna.; Telephone.

Schmitt, Warren.   11 September 1989. Morgantown, Penna.

Skoda, Michael.   26 February 1989. Fort Lauderdale, Fla.; Telephone.

Summers, William.   August 1993. Roanoke, Va.; 285th Reunion.

Wendt, Walter.   17 June 1988. Appleton, Wis.

Zach, Henry.   1 June 1988. Danbury, Wis.; Telephone.

INDEX